AS SEEN ON TV
SOAP SUDS

Edited

By

TRUDI RAMM

First published in Great Britain in 1993 by
ARRIVAL PRESS
1 - 2 Wainman Road, Woodston,
Peterborough, PE2 7BU

Foreword

Originally, this book was to be about television in general. However, after taking a closer look at the poems to be considered, I found that to do the writers justice, I would have to split their work into more specific categories - *As Seen On TV - Soap Suds* is part of the result.

I always knew that Soaps were popular, you only need to look at the television ratings to work that out! But, it wasn't until I actually started editing the poems that I realised just how popular!

As you read through this book, you will find that *Coronation Street* is the most liked programme and *Reg Holdsworth* of *Bettabuys* fame is the character who most engages our sympathy, having said that, most other Soaps are mentioned, including the now defunct *Crossroads* and *Eldorado*.

Regardless of whether you are a closet Soap watcher or an avid fan, you will recognise many familiar faces, places and events within the pages of this book. Maybe this will be a book to return to in ten years to see how things have changed in the world of television Soaps!

Trudi Ramm
Editor

Contents

Bet Lynch - Gilroy

She's solid brass with a heart of gold,
When she was formed God broke the mould.
Bottle blonde, bright pink lips
Earrings swing; so do her hips!

Her name is Bet by now you've guessed.
You'll know that smile, you've seen that chest!
The brightest star on TV,
Her wit can shake the strongest knee.

Behind the laughter there's been tears
And tragedy in her younger years.
A son was taken in his prime,
Steps of sorrow she had to climb.

Lovers come and win her heart,
Steal a kiss and then depart.
Is she broken, sad and bitter?
Not on your life! She's no quitter!

Bets reached the top in her profession,
Through energy, guts and aggression.
Her name's above the *Rover's* door,
Carved with pride for ever more.

When times are hard and tempers short,
Inflation high, finances fraught;
Switch on your set, put up your feet,
There's someone you ought to meet.

Behind a bar she plays her part,
Nimble-witted, wise and smart.
Three cheers for Bet the Queen of Soap.
By her example we can cope.

Jill Johnson

1

Alf Roberts

I'd like a life of leisure *luv*
If it could be with you
I'd even sell the shop
If it could make our dream come true.
I've tried my hand at everything,
From Councillor to Cop;
But in the end - I know I'm just
The owner of a shop.

I've tried to be excited
Over stock and layout too,
But all that keeps me going
Is the thought of life with you.
I like a good old gossip
And with customers I'll chat,
But surely there is something
More to life than all of that.

I've worked hard as a Councillor,
Please folks give me my due;
But everything I've taken on
Has only been for you;
Now, since my heart's not what it was
I'm running out of time
I need to save my energy
To reach the heights sublime.

The shop has been my life 'til now,
Some say the death of me,
But since the day we met Audrey
Nowt does compare with thee!

Rosemary Bellett

Neighbours

Neighbours - who needs noisy nosy neighbours
With their prying and their scheming
They can be perfect fiends.

Neighbours - are the first to turn against us
The first we need to mistrust
With their selfishness and greed.

Neighbours - be it person, group or country
Worker, yuppy, gentry
With hateful neighbours, life's one long scream!

Jack Sharpe

Day Dreaming

Now I'm not particular about drinking myself,
Although I would partake to drink somebody's health.
I go inside a public house five days of the week.
Just to see what friendly people I can seek.
I go inside the 'Woolpack Inn' down near 'Emerdale Farm'
Now that Frank Tate, he drinks too much
He'll do himself some harm.
When entering the 'Rovers Return'
I don't find the men there good looking.
Tho' I do like Betty Turpin who is pleasantly plump,
I could always sit down to her cooking,
Now, I prefer it at the 'Queen Vic'
The Eastenders are natural and real,
I could sit there all night with a drink in my hand.
As long as I could ogle at Phil.
So good looking . . . what a charmer,
His manners are pleasant you see;
If that Sharon can't make up her mind about him.
He can always come round to see me.
He could whisk me up and take me away
To the top of a far off hill,
Then we could be there all on our own,
Just me and the moonlight and Phil.
Now I think it is time that I came down to earth,
Back to reality.
You can't blame me dreaming,
This is no teenage crush,
As I'm a great Grandma you see.

J Short

Bet

Those pints she pulls, as punters sweat or drool
Over a pair of busty boobs, bigger than Liverpool.
Bleached blonde hair and her painted masked face
She can deliver pints faster than Lester could win the Grand National
Race.

Behind her script lines, this blonde can act
and dish out better than she ever got back.
Many a man fell into her trap, for this Lady never knew tact,
Cross this blondeshell punters did learn
They never entered back into the Rovers Return.
She can put a punter back into his place, with a word right vile
Or with a flashing wicked smile.
Many a shiver went down a spine,
As dirty minds drank beer in fear
She was known as the *Queen*
And flashed her boobs on to the TV screen
She can swing those hips, flash that smile
Calm her hot punters with a cold glance,
And hold them in a trance
Her hard blue eyes could tell a sad long tale,
Of love affairs she had, that failed.
Her vibrant character upset many a poor punter's wife
And her red long nails tore into a many a foe's face to bits
Alas their husband dared kiss her ripe inviting pink lips
The loneliness of this blond behind the bar,
Melted many a heart near or far.
Behind her farce hid a hurt blonde,
That only to one man wanted to belong.
She became television's most popular character on the TV set
As mass of her fans sit down to watch Coronation Street,
Rovers Return and our beloved Bet . . .

Diane Full

5

Annie and Bet

A well know pub in Weatherfield
Named the Rovers Return
Ruled by Annie Walker
Steely eyed and stern.
But a lady was our Annie, real name Doris Speed.
A trooper to the very end, on her epitaph you'll read.
Then along came Bet barmaid that was in Coronation Street
Earrings dangling down a mile
Rose red lipstick, great big smile.
Now lots of folk have kidded Bet, tried every trick that's in the book,
But our Bett's got them dangling like fishes on the hook.
So lets drink a toast to Bet and all the rest
Down Coronation Street you simply are the best.

F Twohey

6

Untitled

It's half past one, the housework's done,
Now I'll relax and have some fun.
For Jim to appear. He's just great.
Someone I could call my mate.
He's tall and handsome, so debonair
Oh! to put my fingers thro' his hair
I've watched him as he's got older
Might I say a little bolder.
As husband, widower, lover and Dad,
Sometimes he's happy, sometimes he's sad.
I hope he will never leave the street
If he does I'm sure to weep!
Ramsey Street will never be the same
Who will the neighbours have to blame
He speaks his mind, but always kind.
My poem is finished all is done.
Who is my character - Jim Robinson.

Peggy Cox

Emmerdale

Down on the farm the sheep do bleat
But poor Joe's face, makes me weep
No true mate, to help him smile
A glimpse of a female once in a while.
Poor Joe say's I. Poor Joe indeed
Lonely there only animals to feed
He's taken himself many a wife
They have only caused him strife.
Poor Joe I say. Poor Joe indeed.
Give me a call, I'll fill your need!

M Tregear

Brookside of Bareside

Ron Dixon is the talk of the town
On DD's face you see a frown.
Need you ask who put it there
With her short skirt, thighs quite bare.
Bev doesn't care, nor does Ron
While their liaison carries on and on.
He chases Bev around the shop
Just doesn't know when to stop.
Then taking Ron by the hand
To her flat they will land.
She will have her wicked way
For Ron, afraid it makes his day.
What will happen to poor DD
Will Ron repent. Have to wait and see.

I K Skinner

Hilda Ogden

Oh! Dear Hilda where have you gone?
Your missed such a lot when the *Street* is on,
Bustling about, no time to dream,
Cleaning your house, At Number Thirteen.

How you loved that mural above the fireplace,
The three ducks in flight, and your bright cheery face
When you found a bit of gossip to spread about,
Then find the nearest person to tell or shout.

Shopping, cooking, cleaning at the Rovers,
Remembering when you and Stan were lovers,
Then you come back down to earth with a jolt,
When Stan says 'Hilda pass me the salt.'

Headscarf on, curlers in your hair,
A smudge of pink lipstick, so you look debonair,
Then you go to work, maybe finishing at five,
Singing as you go, *The Hills are Alive*.

Just a bit of scandal here and there,
Kept Hilda happy, and so beware
When you have a secret, keep it to your chest,
For if Hilda's about, she will tell all the rest.

So Hilda, please come back in the *Street*
There are a few new people that you should meet,
That need to be kept on their toes,
So will you come back, who knows?

Sandie J Hutchinson

10

Hilda Ogden

If you walked down the street
past number thirteen,
a headfull of curlers
could often be seen.
Twitching the curtains
an ear to the wall,
the best loved busybody
of them all.
        That's Hilda!

She would gather her gossip
and a bit more besides,
she sang as she cleaned
where the street resides.
Her heart was of gold
of that there's no doubt,
though times could be tough
and at Stan she would shout.
        That's Hilda!

But alas Stan died
leaving Hilda alone,
how would she cope?
without someone to moan.
But there was always the Rovers
she could talk all night,
love her or leave her
there was no one quite like
        Our Hilda!

June H Roberts

Reg Holdsworth

With his colourful glasses
And chirpy little voice
Mr Reginald Holdsworth
Has got to be first choice.

His boldness with the ladies
And happy childlike smile
Always gives amusement
When I watch TV a while.

Will he every marry
Imagine if you can
A life of fun and laughter
With this lovely little man.

He'd like to be redundant
So he can buy the corner store
When Alf and Audrey Roberts
Leave the street for ever more.

Bettabuys was his first love
He made it very plain
Now he'd like to leave there
And start all over again.

I can't help it when I see him
Whenever the *street* is on
he's certainly a dead ringer
for an older Elton John.

Linda Fallen

Dot Cotton

Tall, too thin, Dot scurries about the square
Clutching her shopping bag, headscarf round her hair.
A sad, funny figure, on her way to work - you bet!
Doing others' washing in the local launderette.
Yet, Dot is an original from a very special mould,
Outwardly a gossip, but her heart is purest gold.
Quick to spread a rumour but then first to lend a hand
Dot's a typical Eastender - the backbone of the land.
If I could rub Aladdin's lamp on our Dot's behalf
I would ask the genie to give her a good laugh. My second wish must
be that she gets a decent man.
Rich, tall, good looking with a gorgeous bronze suntan.
Lastly I wish she enjoys a healthy, peaceful life
and puts behind her all her previous strife.
Yet, if I asked Dot what she wants her answer would come quick.
'Nothing for me dearie - save it for my Nick.'

Patsy Brewer

13

He's the Man

He's the man everyone loves to hate
He's the man who decides their fate
He's there to make sure when you fall
You'll never again stand up tall.
He's sly, cunning, devious too
He'll take your love then laugh at you.
He thrives when you hate him, he'll laugh when your sad,
He just doesn't care
He loves being bad.
From seduction to blackmail
This man is relentless,
His power is control
When you are defenceless,
In business the rules are made by him
That's because he has to win.
He has no morals ethics, yet
Still people think that he's a safe bet.
He always makes sure he has something brewing
You must have guessed
It's J R Ewing.

Pamela Shaw

14

Seth of Emmerdale

Seth! Seth! you're not here again,
Drinking in the Woolpack
'Cause it's starting to rain.
Have you no work to go to?
I'll 'ave a pint Mr Turner.
Oh just wait in the queue.
Me mouth's gone dry,
It's me lunch hour Mr Turner,
Was up crack a dawn I'll not tell a lie.
I've been down the fish farm
And fed them fishes,
I work very hard to carry out yer wishes,
I've mended the fence,
Them 'erons won't be back,
And for tea tonight
There's a rabbit in me sack.
Oh take it away I don't want that here,
All that mess and fur in the beer.
Are you ready for the shoot?
It must go OK
There's a lot of wealthy people all willing to pay.
Don't panic Mr Turner, gere me a pint,
I'll check all is well
Tomorrow first light.
Oh. hurry up Seth, I haven't all day,
On your bike you're blocking the way.
If Meg was here she'd give you what for,
Now move it Seth out of that door.
Who'd be a gamekeeper working for 'ee
I'd best go 'ome. It's time for me tea.

Jane Roberts

Pauline Fowler's Cardigan

Pauline's cardigan seems to me
to be worn from morning 'til night,
In every situation that occurs
It turns up looking dowdy and tight.

No wonder Arthur's eyes have strayed
His new love looks very smart.
No cardigan beige and frayed
He's fallen in love with all his heart.

Arthur does not know what to do,
Pauline even wears it in bed,
Every day he is getting blue,
He wishes he had fled.

How long can the cardigan appear
When we turn Eastenders on,
Hopefully the moths will come,
and then it will be gone.

Maureen Swain

A Vignette of Vera

The Duckworths live at number nine,
With Vera, clad in pink and lime.
Her husband Jack, is a lazy slob.
Barman at the Rovers Return is his job.
Her hair is frizzy, her house a mess.
She worked at Betterbuys, got food for less.
Her husband kept pigeons, to her dismay,
But her Daughter-in-law made him give them away.
She has a son, Terry, but he is in jail.
His crime was so bad that he didn't get bail.
Her best friend Ivy lives next door
She's a regular churchgoer, abides by the Law.
Vera has a big mouth and a Yorkshire tone,
Which soon disappears when she speaks on the 'phone.
Every evening she goes for a drink
And piles up the pots in the kitchen sink.
She puts on her lipstick and spruces her hair,
Then goes to the Rovers, because Jack works there.
She orders a drink, a lager or shandy,
Then listens to Jim whilst he moans about Andy.
She bellows at Jack to fetch her two beer
And fiddles about with the hoops in her ears,
Then straightens the scarf that is pushed in her hair.
And checks that her handbag is still on her chair.
Late at night before going to bed,
She fixes two rollers to the front of her head.
After locking the doors and drinking her tea,
She says, 'Goodnight Jack,' and he says, 'Night V!'

Lisa Brownlow

Our Mavis

Of all the many characters that folk would like to meet
Would surely be *Our Mavis* from Coronation Street.

With her job in Rita's *Kabin*, and as dear old Derek's wife,
Her life is full of ups and downs with laughter and some strife.

Her saying 'I don't really know!' to Rita is well known
And her popularity has blossomed, flowered and even grown.

She gives us things to smile about, and sometimes shed a tear
And we hope she will be with us for many a long year.

So give three cheers for Mavis, who gives us such a treat.
And long may she continue in Coronation Street

Carole Greenberg

Ian Beale

In my eyes I see a star,
Hoping and dreaming the way to the top,
Beeping and boasting in his flash car,
It's Ian Beale, losing his money, he hasn't got far.
Crying for help as he sits in his chair,
Picks up the phone and makes a dare;
The Meal Machine is living in his head.
With a tasty grin
The customers are fed.
People are jealous of his down hill career
Through their curtains in the square they peer.
'Oh my God ! He's got a new suit,'
'That Ian Beale, used to be cute.'

Sophia Brown

19

Our Ron

Good ones come, good ones go
but he's the best of all,
and when we turn to Brookside
Ron Dixons' on the ball.

This leader of the clampets,
he fought the Farnhams well
with wooden fences, skips and junk
but never would Max sell.

His father was a bigamist,
his wife a nervous wreck.
His kids took drugs and thieved a bit,
the Legion's such a trek.

Now Ron has strayed once again,
more serious than before,
so goodbye Jackie, hello Bev,
he's closed the Trading Post door!

Frank and Lynn abandoned him
for sleeping with Lynn's sister.
DD knows. The convent's closed
for now Ron is Bev's mister.

Congrats, Vince Earl, you made it,
to the best soap on the screen.
May your character always be,
like Moby Dick, Supreme.

Marian Aherne

Love on an Allotment!

Arthur Fowler - what a cad, playing about like Jack-the-Lad,
In and out of Christine's bed, and she making sure that he's well fed!
Pauline, his wife is so naive, the goings on would not believe.
What happens in the allotment shed, would really make her turn her
head.

In woolly jumper, shirt and tie and creased up trousers pulled up
high,
He goes out, Christine to meet, trying to creep along the street.
Outside the Vic, he has been seen, 'Hello Dad, where have you
been?'
His daughter Michelle wants to know, and that's made his face go
red and glow
He splutters forth some stupid patter, like 'Just popped out for a pint
and a natter'
'With whom?' his daughter asks again, 'Dad don't you know it's half
past ten.'
'Oh, I thought it was only eight, didn't realise it was so late.'
Christine peeped out from cafe door, and was upset with what she
saw.
Michelle then led her Dad back home, once inside he reached for the
'phone
'Christine love - it's only me, I tried to see you, honestly,'
Pauline rose from out of bed and quietly down the stairs did tread,
'Is that you Arthur, who's on the 'phone, I didn't know that you were
home.
I thought you were still at the Vic,' how can Pauline be so thick!
Dear old Arthur you really must, try and curb your fervent lust,
Because between lover and your wife, this carry on will lead to strife.
I know we all just wait to see, what next will happen in this game with
three.
But Pauline is out to catch you out and then you know she'll scream
and shout
So watch it Arthur, keep aware, before you are caught in this affair,
Stay with Pauline and be good, and act like all good husbands
should.

Wendy Ellis

Sharon of Eastenders

What ever type of woman is she
around the Vic she flirts
always in black stockings
and her short black mini skirts.

Shethinks she's just so perfect,
with all her make up on
dyed blond hair and false smile
we know it's all a con.

First she married Grant
but then she went for Phil
now she's moving on Grant again
she thinks it such a frill.

So when you watch Eastenders
and see Sharon start to beg
it won't for Phil or Grant
but nice old Doctor Legg.

D T Champion

Vera Duckworth

Vera Duckworth what a lady
Married to Jack and she's got Terry's baby
I hold my breath and watch the hope
Will she fall apart or will Vera cope.

Irene Emslie

Our Ena

Hair net, and glass of stout,
A face that couldn't look meaner,
Any secrets, she'd find out,
Then try to help - would Ena.

She made the chapel sparkle bright,
To touch it, no vandal would dare,
Played the organ with a touch so light,
Perhaps the angels listened there.

A heart of gold, a hard exterior,
Appearing as such was quite a feat.
As Mrs Sharples she was superior,
To anyone else in Coronation Street.

O Edwards

24

Percy Sugden

Poor Emily they often say
She puts up with Percy every day.
He's not a bad sort, so it seems
But he's hardly the man of a woman's dreams.
He's always right of course it's true,
He thinks his wisdom will enlighten you.
Who wants to stand next to him at the bar
His stories go on too long by far.
His life's a book, there to be told.
With lessons to be learnt for young and old.

Elaine Naylor

Percy Sugden

Percy is the peril of Coronation Street
He keeps Emily Bishop on her feet.
He says he was a winner at the battle of Tobruk
But everybody knows he was just an army cook.
When he's in the Rovers he only drinks halves
And when he tells a joke nobody laughs.
He's being chased by a woman called Phyllis
Who says that Percy is top of her love list.
He's commonly known as a sticky beak
Who's told to keep his nose out every week.
Of other people's private affairs
But Percy only does it because he cares.
With his flat cap and polished shoes
He always buts in with his own points of views.
Yes Percy is the peril of Coronation Street
He always keeps everyone on their feet.

Peter Dolby

26

Jack Duckworth

Poor Jack nagged from morn 'til night
He really is a sorry sight.
Dejected face and broken glasses
Tries to smile at the lasses.
Bets on horses, he hopes will win
While he's pouring out the gin.
Away from Vera he dreams for a while
Another man would run a mile.
Taking orders from the lady boss
Makes him surly, makes him cross.
Pulling the pints, cleaning the bar,
Will never get him very far.
A kiss and smile would be a treat.
For Jack Duckworth of Coronation Street.

Monica Ebbs

Percy Sugden - The People's Campaigner

Percy's nosy but he's sweet
He lodges with Mrs Bishop just down't street
Phyllis thinks he's kinda neat.
Under his table she'd like her feet!
Percy says 'He's having none.'
He's bigger battles to be won
His achievement list goes on and on
El Alameine to bowling green
Can even cook up great cuisine
Once almost made Carnival Queen!
The smartest gent you've ever seen
Pants well pressed right on the seam
Suited up with shoes all clean
Medals polished 'til they gleam
Out to do battle with the wheel clamping regime
Percy's won so it may seem?
He's off to the Legion to sup and preen!

Angela Maria Wilson

Curly Watts

He's hardly a dreamboat tall and slim
Yet my days are filled with thoughts of him
With a tender heart and love to share
He needs someone who'd really care
He's not too bright, slow in fact,
His redeeming feature is he can act.
His nonchalant air as he shrugs off rebuffs,
Gives lie to the hurt and all that stuff.
But he's undaunted that's for sure,
Why else, would he set out to lure
A girl like Angie - with her strong will
And the looks she gives him fit to kill.
Poor old Curly, he needs mothering
Not with someone who'd rather smother him
I'd like to tell him *buck up lad*
There's no good reason to look so sad,
With a job like yours at *Bettabuys*
and promotion, if the Manager dies,
Then the girls will come running to your every command
And you'll smile to yourself and say 'Aint life grand?'

Edna Butler

Phyllis

Back and forth she wanders, to and fro each day.
Bags galore she carries, they really make her sway.
She can be very bossy, and always thinks she's right.
But if she crosses Percy, he gives her quite a fright.
Everyone will know her, her blue rinse goes quite well,
With her outspoken chatter, and her bossy ways as well.
She must be all of seventy, but to and fro she goes.
There's nothing you can tell her, as everything she knows.
That's not to say her ideas are right, in fact she gets things wrong.
She can cause quite an upset, she causes quite a song.
She can do this, she can do that, always better than most.
But now that Percy has rejected her, she is left with tea and toast.
Don't think Phyllis will win him, but she will do her best
For poor old Percy Sugden is ready for a rest.
He tried to help poor Emily and she has got quite cross
Now do we think that Phyllis at last will be his boss?

S Rippingale

Eldorado

Goodbye Eldorado, all sunny and sandy
So long Serg, Pilar and Marcus Tandy.
Farewell Alex, Trish and Joy
Rosario, Ingrid and her little boy.
Roberto and Maria adieu
Drew and Nessa goodbye too.
Au revoir to Blair and Gwen
Olive and Freddie see you then.
It seems it was a waste of time
But in the rating you were doing fine.
I know I wish they would keep you on
Because I'm going to miss you all when you've gone.

J Leggitt

I'll Miss Marcus Tandy

Some televisions series come,
And some series go,
The one I've been watching
Is the one called, Eldorado.

It takes place in sunny Spain,
Where the beaches are sandy
One of the main characters
Is called Marcus Tandy.

Now Marcus loves and leaves, all the girls,
He is a right, Jack the Lad
He is a loveable rogue with lots of money
But he is portrayed, as being quite bad.

He dabbles in lots of crooked deals
And some of them go wrong,
He is still after Pilar, and wants her back
And hopes, it won't take him too long.

That Marcus Tandy, is so full of charm
He seems to get all that he craves
I'm sure he will let back Pilar
Without making too many waves.

I'm going to miss Marcus Tandy
When it's time for him to go
No more will he be on my TV
They are getting rid of Eldorado.

Stephanie Harvey

Percy Who

Percy is a stubborn guy
Certainly he is never shy
He tries everyone's life to run
And boasts about what he has done.
Both Emily and Phyllis they do suffer
At the attitude of this old duffer . . .

In the Army he was a cookie
Little more than a rookie.
Everyone thinks he is a bore
Self-centred to the very core.
But Percy has another side
Which even he tries hard to hide.

Everyone in Coronation Street
Crosses the road him not to meet
Who is this ogre we love to see
Percy Sugden the busy bee . . .

Kathy Wilkinson

The Street

A never ending jigsaw of colourful folk
Mike Baldwin - the affluent
The Duckworths - so broke!

The years have seen changes
the people we meet
Yet, the core is the same - Coronation Street.

The Rovers Return, the hub of their world
Where the trials and the smiles in their lives are all hurled.
The *greats* that have gone, we will never forget
Like Minnie with Bobby and Ena with net.
We loved *acid tongued* Annie and Bradley the cad
Poor Rita's had husbands, but her life's been so sad.

Mavis and Derek, soul mates I'm sure
I'm so glad that Victor was shown to the door.

There's been Lucille and Harry, Concepta and Ray
If I tried to name all, I'd be here for the day!
Peter Noone, Davy Jones - add a musical feel

To a landmark that's never fake - always so real.

Allyson Peel

Paul Robinson

My name's Paul Robinson
I'm from the famous Neighbours set,
Yep, I live in Ramsey Street
Out of which I've had some stress.

I like my money
Coming in thick and fast,
I own Lassiters business
Which really didn't last.

I've had a lot of bad luck
I can't seem to be right,
I seem to pay more attention,
To my business not my wives.

At one point I went crazy,
And had to go away,
Now I'm back again
Being just the same.

I have a few children
Out of which I live with one,
His name is Andrew
He is Chrissy and mine's son.

I need a break now,
I'm leaving Ramsey Street
I'll leave all my bad luck behind,
And go to Hawaii with the heat.

Emma Cole

35

The Lovable Rogue

In Emmerdale, Eric Pollard's got to be
The best thing that's ever happened to TV
He's naughty but nice,
And I'd be there in a trice
If he ever came calling on me!

He plays such a contrasting part
Among the jeans and the wellies he's smart
In his neat tie and suit
He looks kinda cute
No wonder he's captured my heart.

I'm pleased that he's now settled down,
(He has been a bit of a clown)
But Elizabeth beware
If I'm ever over there
I might lure him out on the town!

P Lane

36

Curly Watts

Curly Watts
What a lad,
He's not bad
Want's a nice girl
Who'll be his pearl
A good father he would make
If only to give him a break
I'd like to see him have the chance
If only they'd let him have a good romance.

P Bury

The Brookside Cast

I've got a little tale to tell
About some scousers you know so well.
For Lyn and Frank it's the final straw
To see Bev flirt with the man next door.
Bev and Ron are years apart.
But only in age and not with the heart
Come on now Ron don't cheat on your wife
Without DD you have no quality of life.
Maxi has always got plenty to say
While Suzannah is still in the US of A
With three noisy kids that is no joke
Patsy's off on business leaving poor Max to cope
Barry's got a problem at night club *La Luz*
And Jimmy can't help he's got enough to do
For money lovely Anna's turned into a tart
It's not worth it though, Peter tell her to be smart
Money's not everything as Sinbad does know
A window cleaner now laying a patio.

Clair Eaton (16)

38

Untitled

Oh how do you wash your hair Curly?
Oh how do you wash your hair?
'Cause greasy's the way I'd describe it Curly
Greasy beyond compare.
But surely your name is Norman, Curly
Oh surely Curly it is
Norman suits you better Curly
Boring, shy a misfit
I shouldn't take the micky Curly
I shouldn't take the mick
'Cause I really love you Curly.
Unlike the other girls you pick
Angie, Raquel and Kimberley just
Aren't worth your time
Because my dear, dear, dear Curly,
You are just divine.

Claire Coker (13)

Percy

You know too much
You know it all!
You speak your mind
Drive us up the wall.

You're honest though
You're oh so true
Pity not to Phyllis
Who so loves you.

You're the perfect gent
And a little saint
You're heaven sent
We find it quaint.

You upset folks with
your standards high,
To all others
They're pie in the sky!

You're outmoded Perce
With your wartime tales
But if all had your morals
There'd be less in our jails!

S M Ibbotson

I Love Reggie Holdsworth

Oh, I love Reggie Holdsworth,
Although he's short and stout,
I'd do without my groceries,
If Betterbuys threw him out.

Yes, I know he wears glasses,
That hide his bluish eyes,
And that he's no Mel Gibson,
But Oh, he makes me sigh.

Oh, Reg has dreams of greatness,
Perhaps The Street's too small,
But to take away my dumpy jewel,
Would spoil crown, Coronation, and all!

Oh Reg, Oh Reg, for one wobbly smile,
I'm sure I could walk, nearly a mile.
But I fear you'll marry and leave,
Oh, and then will I grieve,
For my best, best Betterbuys Boy!

Jacqueline Hall

Reg Holdsworth

Our Reg is such a character
In Coronation Street.
To see him wooing Maureen
Is really quite a treat.
At every turn he's thwarted
By her mother on the phone.
He never seems to get his
Lovely Maureen on her own.
One night we watched with bated breath
When she went to Reg's home.
And into bed he got her
At last they were alone.
The water bed went up and down
It gave us quite a thrill.
Then all at once fate stepped in
Derek Wilton with his drill.
With water all around the place
Mavis and Derek looking on.
Maureen ran off home to Mum
We thought poor Reg, she's gone.
But now she has consented
To become our Reg's wife.
We know they will be happy
Throughout their married life.
We anxiously are waiting
We hope that they won't tarry.
For we can hardly wait to see.
Reg and Maureen marry.

C M Bent

Duckworth's Lot

Another crate from the cellar Jack,
Did tha' hear what I say?
Bets face is set like concrete.
Tha's not in here to play.
He gamely goes about his work
Until the end of shift draws nearer.
Then Bet Gilroy's had her pound of flesh
And it's home to fearsome Vera.
He greets her in his customary optimistic way
How is little Tommy and is there owt to eat today?
He must wonder where it all went wrong
Who wrote this flaming plot?
They should change the title of the show
And call it Duckworth's lot.

Sam Spruce

43

Tribute to Reg

Without him the series would not be complete
Our loveable Reggie who lives down the street
His long suffering underling young Curly Watts
Must obey without question when Reg calls the shots.

Now Reg has a sweetheart for him there's no other
He's even prepared to put up with her mother.
He pursued his beloved with a passion unique
But his ardour was dampened when his bed sprung a leak.

Humiliated, hurt, his true love fled the scene
This was the last straw for our scatty Maureen
But Reg battled on and he swallowed his pride
And Maureen accepted, yes! she would be his bride.

Redundancies threatened and Reg had a plan
he'd buy out Alf Roberts and be his own man
he made Alf an offer a bargain was struck
Then fate took a hand and Reg ran out of luck.

He went back on his offer tried reducing the bid
Alf wouldn't agree no, not even a quid
When Reg thought it over he knew he was beat
he returned to the shop and admitted defeat.

I'll give you your money, I'll give you the lot
You're too late said Alf, I've sold it to Scott
Reg glared at Brendan his enemy of old
He'd got his redundancy and Reg hadn't been told.

With dreams all in tatters and tears in his eyes
It looks like his future is at Battabuys
So good luck to Reg, let's hope wedding bells chime
And please let him stay with us for a very long time.

Peter Burton

He was There

He was there for sorting Grant out
When he hurled himself around.
He was there to comfort Sharon
When Grant knocked her to the ground.
He was there to help behind the bar
And keep the clients happy.
He was there to give advice to Grant
When Sharon was unhappy.
He was there to help save her life
This really seemed the end.
He was there to put the fire out
Their truest, truest friend.
He was there when the police arrived
To take away his brother.
He was there with shoulder strong and firm
He cradled Sharon like a brother.
He was there when temptation caught them both
Though they tried to hide their feelings.
He was there when they ignored her marriage vows
What a shame their heads were reeling.
He was there for them both all the time
And now Grant is home he feels outshone.
He is still there to give both of his best
To take all the hurt, for Grant must never catch on.
He is there with his heart crying, 'Please help me.'
Write *happy* for *Phil* - you must can't you see?
Put him there again with a new love . . . hear my plea!

K E Sanderson

Reg Holdsworth

You look so smart and hunky,
As you strut around the store,
Muscles, firm and chunky,
Who could ask for more?
If only I could work for you,
Oh, to catch a glimpse each day,
I'd fill the shelves, tins, two by two,
In that perfect *Bettabuys* way,
You'd watch me, as I worked the till,
I know you like to tease,
Your smile gives me such a thrill,
Reg, 'Give me a job please!'

A Dancy

Alma Sedgewick

A lovely star, so pretty to see
Is none other than Amanda Barrie
In *The Street* she's married to Mike
He's the one, we all dislike.

She's called Alma and she works with Gail
With pies and cakes that are for sale
With her large expressive eyes
Men want more than just her pies.

But if they so much as look at the lass
They will probably be hit by flying glass
'Cos Mike has wed her, and so she's his
None but him can give her a kiss.

He's now introduced her to his son Mark
That must have surely left its mark
Again she feels like second best,
Playing second fiddle like all the rest.

But Alma needn't feel so insecure
'Cos she's better than Mike that's for sure
She's as straight as a dye, with heart of gold
To stand up to Mike she needs to be bold.

One day he will go too far again
And he'll fill her golden heart with pain
She'll cry and rage, and tell Rita her woes
But we hope she doesn't tear up his clothes.

Remember the time, she tore the bed sheets to bits
When she had one of her jealous fits
When Mike had left her for that Jackie
But to tear the bed sheets, that was tacky.

But we all love Alma that's for sure
We hope she goes on year after year.

Irene Woodcock

The Greatest Guy

I have watched you from a far,
A great talented TV star
You have always been my secret lover
Although you have let Pauline down for another
But how I wished that it was me
That you were coming round to see
When is Pauline going to find you out
And pack your bags and turn you out.
Will Christine ever be sure
You will keep to her for ever more
Or are you just playing her about
If I was *them* I would not give a toss
And both show you they are the boss
Arthur Fowler this refers to you:
Yes you could always live with me
But I am sure in reality behind the scenes
You would not do these nasty things
I'll bet you are the greatest guy, husband and dad
That anyone could ever have
I will still keep watching you with glee
As Eastenders is the best for me.

V Davies

Down on the Street

From down on the Street, he's one of the guys,
He is boss at the store they call Bettabuys,
Mr Curly Watts plays his loveable sidekick,
He is lanky, and gawky, really quite thick.

The love of his life is the nervous Maureen,
With the most interfering mother you've ever seen,
Though she was unsuccessful in spoiling their fate,
For he romantically went and set the date.

He has booked the wedding for a day in September
It will be a day they will all remember,
All are invited the young and the old
Gossip and stories are sure to be told.

His rival in business runs the corner shop,
And in competition, at nothing they'll stop,
But with his supermarket he has the edge,
And always takes home the biggest wedge.

Down at the Rovers, he enjoys a few drinks,
With all of the regulars, his friends he thinks,
Some like him yes but others don't know,
He is quite a character and puts on a show.

It's true to say that since he joined the cast,
It's lively and funny at a pace that's quite fast,
He is funny and witty with a humour so dry,
He leaves you with many a tear in your eye.

So keep it up Reggie, you really make the Street
Entertainment and viewing that's very hard to beat.

Debbie Griffen

Caught Out

Neighbours? Never watch it
The worst thing on TV
What's that? You've seen me watching?
Never! No! Not me!

Who's that *Jim* they talk about?
Not bad for an older man.
And who on earth are the Willises?
Dotty Doug and poor old Pam.

They tell my Lucy has run off
And left broken hearted Brad
I'm also told that poor old Todd
Was going to be a dad.

Madge? Who's she? I don't know her.
Wears lovely frocks I'm told
And never has one hair out of place
Why does she never look old?

Now *Honest Lou* now there's a man
They tell me he's quite a guy
But *Honest* well I'm not so sure,
From him a used car I'd not buy!

Helen's had her ups and downs
Or so my friends tell me!
But she's always there with a casserole
And lots of sympathy.

Oh No! you've caught me watching
But I'm just trying to see,
What all the fuss is about,
Then, darling, I'll cook your tea!

Amanda Smith

51

Dear Sharon - c/o The Queen Vic

Now Sharon dear, it's very clear,
You're not sure what you're doing:
One minute Grant is number one,
The next it's Phil you're wooing.

But when it came to telling Grant
How much you loved his brother,
You changed your mind, and dropped poor Phil
In favour of the other.

No wonder Phil looks so confused;
he's had no luck with love,
And Grant keeps saying, all the time,
'Be happy for me, Bruv.'

It's just as well Grant doesn't know
About your fling with Phil -
Things would be worse than when he flipped,
And beat up the old bill.

So Sharon dear, I hope you know
You could be in for trouble;
With brothers like those Mitchell boys
The trouble would be double.

Gaelyn Jolliffe

Jason Donovan

He made his name on BBC 1
He played in Neighbours as Scott Robinson
He thrilled both Madge and Harry,
For their daughter, he did marry,
This joyful day, fans won't forget,
The dripping hankies, soaking wet,
Later they moved off the set,
To produce a little Jasonette.

He left Neighbours and topped the charts,
With a song entitled *Too Many Broken Hearts*,
He appeared on Top of the Pops live,
Several times reaching the top five,
He made a hit with Kylie too,
A duet *Especially for You*.

He moved to the theatre and again was a big hit,
He played Joseph in his multicoloured kit,
He's done the chat shows too, but as a guest,
But right now he's taking a well earned rest.

Deborah Jones

Untitled

There is one programme
That's hard to beat
Coronation Street
Three times a week.

The stars work hard
And do their best
Keeping the Street
Ahead of the rest.

Bridget C Squire

The Queen from the Vic

It may be heard that Sharon's a fool
From those louts across the square
But since time began, it seems to me
Shaz has always been there.

Her dad is pushing up flowers
Angie's flown to Spain
Not a great picture of family life
But Sharon still remains.

Angie and Den have flown the nest
Leaving Sharon all alone
But does she leave to start again
She runs the pub all on her own.

Grant and Phil try desperately
But surely to no avail
Sharon's heart is set on the Vic
Serving lager, beer and ale.

To those who ask the question of
Who is the best Eastender?
The only answer is the one of
Sharon, without contender.

Peter Starkey

Dot

There she is, with furrowed brow,
It wouldn't seem the same somehow
If dear old Dot should disappear
From the *soap* we hold so dear.
Always ready to lend a hand
Always trying to understand.

Her wayward son has caused such stress
But she stands by him nonetheless.
Her faith is strong - it sees her through
Her troubled life, and good times too.
With fag in mouth and ears alert
For any gossip others may blurt.

Our Dot continues day to day
Grateful for all that comes her way.
A heart of gold - she cares for any
Who need a home - and there've been many
Who've turned to her when times were bad,
And found the *mum* they never had.

Oh yes, she's prudish and likes things right,
But all have good points in her sight.
She can see the best in folk
When others only fun will poke.
She's nosy, and loves tales to tell,
But Albert Square knows that so well!

With all her faults, she's well respected
Without her there, they'd feel dejected.
A *character* in many ways,
So, Dot, for your remaining days,
Please stay on screen - we'd miss you so,
If you ever decided to go.

G Whittle

56

Our Bet

She's a legend to all on the Street where she lives,
Her talent, her wit, she generously gives,
Whether hair piled on high or tied with a bow
Our message to Bet is *we all love you so.*

She's had her fair share of heartache and pain,
But comes back on top again and again.
With long dangly earrings and red ruby lips
Not to mention those curvy and shapely hips.

Though mostly portrayed as brassy and bold,
it's hard to disguise that heart of gold,
When the chips are down and problems crop up
It's hard to resist it when Bet says 'Sup up.'

She's loved and she's laughed, been happy, been sad,
But all through the years never really been bad
She leaves all her viewers with courage and hope
The main ingredients that make a good soap.

The *Rovers Return* a most popular bar,
Would not be the same without Bet as its star
Our thoughts and our prayers all go with you Bet
To millions of viewers we hope its still on *the set.*

Amen, so be it, Auf Wiedersehen Pet
May good luck and happiness always follow you Bet,
Be it *on the street* or in places unknown
We will never forget you, wherever you roam.

Mabel Pattison

Reg Holdsworth

As I sit down
And put pen to paper
I'm watching my favourite show
It's not that
The programmes a caper
It's *Reg* that just makes it glow.

Whether he's on
For ten minutes or two seconds
He's professional with all of his lines
The delivery is
All that one reckons
He makes me feel great, he just shines.

His obvious charm
And that face splitting smile
Are two of his many attractions
Reg isn't glum
It's just not his style
Even if it's a faulty transaction.

Lets hope that
The *Street* in its foresight
Gives the Bettabuys Boss many a gag
For Ken Morely
A star·in his own right
Will ensure audiences never flag.

Ron Marriott

Sundown

Goodbye then Eldorado
Stanley, Freddie and Miss King,
all moving on to play
in some other thing.

Pilar, Marcos, Giogio - unhappy three
it all ended in tears, it had to be -
Alex married Trish and,
we'll never know for sure
who left poor Joy upon the bar room floor.

Gwen, Drew and the awful Blair -
Nessa came from we don't know where,
Bunnie lost his Fizz, Rosario her Son
Roberto got a shock and Trine had fun,
but she almost lost her Mum and Dad
as well as any innocence she might have had.

Ingrid gave birth, what else could she do?
But Grandma didn't say a word the whole thing through.
The Hindle boys left early, one lost his wits,
Jerrie fought on longer then called it quits.
So farewell Los Bacos, I think it's a shame
we'll not see the urbanisation again,
if Aunty Beeb had kept her nerve I know
Eldorado had the makings of a decent show.

E R Brush

Ode to Marcus Tandy

Perfection, Oh not Marcus he's sexy and he's bad,
But underneath the badness he's just a little sad.
I look into the deep dark eyes, my soul is set on fire,
With promises, oh promises, so full of strong desire.
A sigh escapes his pouting lips, lips I yearn to kiss.
A happiness that lingers there, to grab and not to miss.
I long to run my fingers through his hair so thick and black
And travel on love's journey to eternity and back.
He's everything I dream of, alas my heart is lost.
So I'm leaving for Los Bacos, and never mind the cost.

Sherridan Gregory

Jack and Vera

Down the road,
      or a little nearer
Sits the abode,
      of Jack and Vera.
Smell the sizzling bacon,
      and hear the laughing lad.
Then Vera flips,
      because Jack just makes her mad.

Jack's into horses,
      cards and drink
And Vera's into,
      causing a stink.
With Jack's pigeons,
      being his pride
Vera's stuck
      alone inside.

Jack pulls pints,
      instead of lasses.
He's overweight
      and needs new glasses.
Vera's raucous,
      brassy and bold
But dear Vera's
      got a heart of gold.

Little Tommy's,
         spoilt rotten
Jack is jealous
         and feels forgotten.
So if one day
         you're out gadding,
You should spot
         their stone cladding,
And raised voices
         on drawing nearer
You can bet,
         it's Jack and Vera.

Amanda Druce

Dirty Den Strikes Again

I'm writing my poem about dirty Den
He is one of life's most adorable men
'Cause all the games and tricks he's played
You can honestly see why Eastenders was made.

Den and Angie are a really great pair
Pity he couldn't show her how much he could care
For all the women in his life
There's no-one really like his wife.

He thought he really loved our Jan
Pity he wasn't her type of man
Now back to Angie in a dream
You'd thought he was the cat that got the cream.

Den Knows a lot of Walford thieves
Even the mob we were lead to believe
No-one knows how he died that day
Even the script writers will not say.

The show isn't the same, now our Den's gone
They have changed the theme, but not the song
He's a very good actor you cannot deny
It's a pity his character had to die.

S J Mantle

63

Mandy - A True Eastender

There is a girl called Mandy loiters round Albert Square
Who's trouble-making dishonesty is enough to make you swear.
She'll steal your milk and money too, then ask you for a job,
'I've nowhere to live, please take me in,' said with heart-rending sob.

You take her in and help her, but she wants and takes much more,
By the time she's finished with you, you're showing her the door.
You may wonder who this Mandy is the cause of many a frown.
Well, you'll find someone just like her in any City or Town.

You can see her twice a week if only you switch on,
Tuesday's and Thursday's 7.30 on BBC 1
She's played by Nicola Stapleton
She plays her so convincingly with such style and flair.
You'd like to smack her round the face and even pull her hair.

Bill Harris

Dot Cotton

With a fag in one hand, and gossip to tell
Dot visits the Doctor for she is unwell
Her son is in prison, her husband's now dead
Both one big headache it has to be said . . .

Although a strict Christian, life hasn't been fair
She spends all her days washing clothes for the square.
She's had several lodgers like Nigel of late
And enjoys spending time with Ethel her mate.

At the end of the day and sometimes before
Dot meets her neighbours behind the pub door
Their dramas and problems are never concealed
As soon as Dot hears them her mouth can't be sealed.

Helen Clark

Sophie

I like to look at *Home and Away*
But Sophie's a bit much to take.
I know the poor girl's had her problems
And life never seems very fair
But couldn't she just for once
Listen to people who care?
It's always blamed on a childhood
Deprived of care and love -
But since she now has found them
Couldn't her attitude change?
She should be glad of the love she has now
And try to her life rearrange
She can't go wrong with Pippa
Who is nearly always right
Who comes up with the answers
And knows just how to cope
With all the problems thrown at her -
She surely knows the ropes.
It's hard to be a teenage mum
To see your friends have all the fun -
While you have baby to attend
And chores it seems they have no end
You think of all you're missing
The mess you've made of your life
Much better had you waited
'Til you became a loving wife.

E M Wilcox

66

Coronation Character

Percy Sugden tugged on his cap
And went upon his way,
He had to set the world to rights
It must be done today.

By the left! Quick march to the corner shop
To check Alf's sell-by dates,
And then across to the Kabin
Where a nervous Mavis waits.

The shopping done, the brass all clean,
The yard is swept and spotless,
Time to check the Rover's bar
is polished, clean and faultless.

Inspection passed, half of bitter,
Best go muster Mrs B
Disgraceful pavements full of litter,
Never mind! It's shepherds pie for tea.

He's done his duty for his country,
Feeding soldiers under fire,
His gravy it was never lumpy,
Of his Christmas pud they'd never tire.

With moustache bristling, mind alert,
Our Percy champions all,
He will not with our Phyllis flirt
When he hears duty call.

Christine Kelly

Reg Holdsworth

The cat has settled down upon the tiles.
Now for the shifty, double dealing smiles
That cloak this egoistic guy
Who rules the roost at Betterbuys.

Each episode I sit and gaze
At this smug fellow; through a haze
of awe and trembling fear, for what
Script writers in their zeal, have got
for him to do and say.

The betrothal day at last is plighted
Will joy be his or hopes all blighted?
His treatment of Curly,
one can only deplore -
and how will he cope
With a mother-in-law.

How shiftily he eyes his prey,
Like a fat cat with mice at play,
All his plotting, amorous schemes
Collapse as he wakes up from his dreams.
His mattress punctured - how we laughed!
Romeo, oh Romeo - didn't he look daft.

Mary Spencer Brown

Our Vera

A lovely wife, a good mother too
I wonder if it could be true
Always moaning about her Jack
Talking about the neighbours behind their backs.

Jack's off down the Legion but wait a minute here
Jack go to the Rovers I want a glass of beer
Looking after baby Tom, shopping in the town
Can't go to Alf's any more, 'til his prices come down.

In trouble with the boys in blue
No insurance on Emily's car
It's a pity I sold it she said to Jack
Now I can't get far.

Always looking on the bright side
Things will never change
Down in Coronation Street
Where Vera gets her name.

K Cooper

Tinker - The Emmerdale Kitten

Since finding fame in Emmerdale
Young Tinker's in a flap.
They've billed him as a lady cat -
He's certain he's a chap!
They tell him he's a *natural*
Who will gather fans in dozens,
But he'll never hold his head up
With his macho moggy cousins.
Still his bank account looks healthy
Since they cast him as a Doll -
And he'll know he's really made it
When he stars in Cage Aux Folles!

Joan B Howes

Our Hilda

Loving wife of hen-pecked Stan,
Chips a-frying in the pan,
That was Hilda Ogden
Never to be forgotten.

The Street's residing Lady of the Manor
Was a good match for Hilda, in Elsie Tanner,
With slanging matches in the street
Annie Walker could not compete.

Cleaning loos and scrubbing floors
Were just a few of Hilda's chores,
Rover's slapdash, quickflip char,
But ne'er allowed behind the bar.

For her, no slice of honey melon,
Though sometimes, a treat of port and lemon,
Nothing brought her any luck
Not even a china flying duck.

Turban and rollers to the fore
Went very well with her decor,
Her pride and joy was dearest *Murial*
Which should, one day, be her memorial.

A woman happy with her lot,
Buying luxuries, she could not,
She found her *all* in rotund Stan
Her very own nourished *He-Man*.

Her outward ways and rasping tongue
Began to fool not every one,
For underneath that icy cold
There beat a heart of purest gold.

W E Townsend

Coronation Street

Some parts make me laugh some make me cry,
Some parts make me ooh some make me sigh,
Most I love but one or two I hate,
Especially Reg Holdsworth who cannot get a date.

Rita has had her share of trouble,
Her love life is a total muddle,
Bet too behind the bar,
Her blonde hair has not got her far.

The Barlow - Baldwin triangle
In whose life they can wangle,
After all their indefinite loves,
They still wear the boxing gloves.

But Jack and Vera, they are the best,
They put each other to the test,
Now poor Vera is left holding the baby,
Is she happy now, well maybe . . .

C Dodds

Skin Deep

Cuddly Alan Turner
with his fetching dimpled smile
could be quite a lady's man
if he would change his style;
but unless he finds a partner
who loves him, fat and all,
who'll let him do the cooking,
be at his beck and call,
ignores his suspect motives
when doing his good deeds
and knows he's just a lonely man
who cooks and overfeeds,
I fear he'll end up on the shelf
a victim of the devil *self*

So every time I see him
get in another mess
I feel like shouting 'Alan
for goodness sake confess
that you have a problem,
your confidence is nil;
swallow your pride and you will find
it's not a bitter pill;
life is what you make it
and under all that fat
you're really rather special
and I could go for that;
so change your image while you can,
time, you know, waits for no man.'

Eileen M Lund

Phoebe Bright

Poor old Phoebe Bright
Nothing in her life goes right.
First she's deserted by her mum
Then her dad does hit her some,
Next he dies and she's alone
But still she doesn't moan.
She went to live with schoolmarm Dot
And found that Todd cared a lot,
But soon she found she was with child
And seemed to go completely wild.
Todd when getting to her side
Was knocked down and then he died,
Poor Phoebe thought it was the end,
But still she had a child and friend.
The Neighbours they all rallied round
And soon her feet were back on the ground.
Let's hope her life improves now on
And her troubles are all gone.

Tracy Beal

Untitlted

Weatherfield's where it all happens
At the Rovers Return Pub
All the streets problems chewed over
Along with Betty's pub grub.

There's steady Ken Barlow, at odds with Mike
Liz McDonald's twins - not a bit alike
Mavis and Derek who dither along
And Rita whose relationships always go wrong.
There's Jack the barman and Vera his spouse
One up in the street with their stone-cladded house
And dizzy Raquel, a resting model
Who since meeting Gordon, thinks cricket's a doddle.
But, the star of the show is Bettabuys lad
Blue spectacled Reg with his mini and *pad*
His old love Maureen re-entered his life
And now his aim is to make her his wife.
A water bed he hoped would clinch it, who could resist the thrill
But they both came to a watery end when Derek began to drill.
With all this now forgiven, the romance back on course
It's love behind the fixtures, amidst pickles and bottles of sauce.
So here's to the day when cuddly Reg eventually ties the knot
And retires to the corner shop - leaving Curly the blooming lot!

Priscilla M Uren

75

Dallas Days

There's a programme on TV called Dallas
And JR's the baddie, you'll see!
Sue Ellen's a drunk, and Pam's done a bunk
And Bobby came out of the sea.
Miss Ellie she wed Clayton Farlow
One day he'll burst into song
There's Donna and Ray, but they moved away
And Lucy, who can do no wrong.
Now Gary's the family black sheep
In JR's eyes he has no standing
So he moved, and yes, I'm sure you can guess
He started a programme called Knott's Landing.

Agnes Boyd

Hold On Holdsworth

My heart is breaking darling,
Or may I call you Reg?
Forget about that Maureen,
Stick to your meat and veg.

She'll turn out like her mother,
A fruit and nutty case.
I wish you'd take me Reggie,
Pluck me from this human race.

You've had a few flirtations
Down in Coronation Street,
But I think my *Special Offer*
May be very hard to beat

You only have to say the word,
And flash your sexy smile.
Jump in my mobile trolley,
Let me whisk you down the aisle.

I'll pick up all the bargains
You are kind enough to proffer,
And swap my old detergent
Just to be your lover.

We'll make an ideal couple,
Please make me your First Prize
Move over Jack and Vera
Here come the Bettabuys!

A V Heiron

Boring Pauline

Pauline Fowler really is a miff,
Her and Arthur always in a tiff,
Wearing his cardies with such flair,
And what can you say about her hair,
Their marriage really is a joke,
At which people, fun will poke,
Him at the allotment with his greens,
Her at the launderette washing the jeans,
Natter with Pete about his market stall,
Go to give Martin and Vickie a call,
'Mum can you baby-sit tonight,' says Shell with a sigh,
'Course I can luv,' comes her mum's reply,
At the ready with tea on the brew,
Dinner on the stove, oh no not stew!
'Where's that Arthur, late again.'
I just don't know how I keep sane!
Off to the Vic for a drink with Dot,
To hear all the gossip, and what a lot,
Home to Arthur at the end of the day,
There's not much more you can really say!

Jan Lowe

Untitled

He's the barman at the Rovers
Known to all as Jack
One thing he hates is lifting crates
He blames his dodgy back
He doesn't fair much better
When his work is done
'Cos he goes home to Vera
Now that can't be much fun.
She blames him for their troubles
For all their cares and woes
She's always going on at him
to keep him on his toes.
She points out all the faults he has
She could make quite a list
But if he were to leave the street
He would be sadly missed.

H Thorogood

Pilar

Though ill-starred *Eldorado* has breathed its last
        I shall remember Pilar . . .
        Not a star,
        A la Hollywood,
        All pouts and peroxide,
        But fairer by far for that.
        Lustrous hair and eyes
        Glistening like black olives
        And skin as smooth as them,
        Would spread the sun,
        Painfully missing here,
        The one winter *Eldorado*
        Gleamed on our screens.
And, in spite of first halting triteness,
Sped wave-lapped Costa to our fog-feel rooms . . .
        Deep poppy lips
        Framing neat, infant teeth . . .
        (Not your actual *Farrah False Set* rocks)
        Disseminated sweet,
        Flawed English, unspoiled by RADA
        And the shape of a real woman,
        Not an ironing board.
        Laughing girl, you charmed us for a year,
        With your poppy-lipped cry of *Mar-coos!*
        Adios, now, Miss Natural,
        The flower of Los *Bar-coos.*

Edna Harvey

80

Dream Lover

Who is that cheeky cherub
lurking in the fruit and veg
it's the pride and joy of Betterbuys
good old randy Reg,
Casting out far and wide
that well used roving eye
for yet more failed romances
each greeted with a sigh,
But for sheer persistence
the guy must score a ten
knock him down he bounces
straight back up again,
With a dapper line in clothing
and an ample share of charm
finally he's claimed his prize
a lady on his arm,
I refer of course to Maureen
the lady of his dreams
a victim in his wicked web
of dirty plots and schemes
Outwardly this tiger
is just a little kitten
has gone from hard and ruthless
to well and truly smitten.
It's so romantic how he tells her
there will never be another
but his evil mind is thinking
how to get rid of her mother,
But Reg would not be Reg
with no problems in his path
and his attempts to solve them
should at least give us a laugh!

Eric Peters

Dear Bet

I'm not a TV addict,
I like to choose *my stuff*,
But when it's Coronation Street
I'll never have enough.
I've watched it from the very first
So many years ago,
But without Bet Lynch, my favourite,
My telly would have to go.
She's everybody's person,
Posh, common, and a mannequin too,
She puts on the charm, oh so calm,
Then yells and screams at you.
One moment, she's Queen of Sheba
Next a tiger wild,
But she's very fond of children
Especially Alex's grandchild.
When Jack, he goes overboard,
Bet's looks would stop a thief
And even Vera, holds her tongue
When Bet becomes *the chief*.
Her hairdo's are spectacular,
Whenever, night or day
She's always dressed up to *the nines*
As we tend to say.
She also enjoys a crafty puff,
But never in the bar,
Everybody loves dear Bet,
I know that she'll go far.

M Williams

82

Letter to Weatherfield

Dear Jack,
How do you tolerate all that abuse,
From a woman who regards you as obtuse,
Never any cash for a flutter on the nags,
Broken glasses and a paunch that sags
Can't disguise the man inside,
Pushing, determinedly, against the tide.
You dream of wealth and a better life,
And, hopefully, a different wife.
You're a stalwart, Jack, when needs dictate,
But Vera just doesn't appreciate,
What a jewel she's trapped within her stone-clad walls,
Because you're always there when duty calls.

Paul Williams

In Praise of Bet Lynch

Superb, droll, laconic Bet -
Your wit has no peers,
Endearing you to millions,
Evoking mirthful tears.

Your devastating candour -
Delivered thrice per week,
Amuses without rancour -
Lampooning all that's bleak!

Pat McLean

Bet of the Rover's Return

The Rover's Return still proudly stands,
Skilfully run in Bet's capable hands,
She is strong, she is brave, she is loyal and true,
I should like her as friend, after all wouldn't you?
Years passed as her character came on the scene
As a poor little someone scarce out of her teens,
But with inner light burning, courageous and strong
With only commitment to bring her along.
The woman from nowhere is somebody now,
With North Country grit she shows us all how
To climb up the ladder of fortune and fame
And yet just be Bet, who is always the same.
From lonely teenager to everyone's pal -
You have to admit she's one hell of a gal.
For in this tough world where the going is fast
There's no time to cry for mistakes of the past -
For the men that she loved or the child that she lost,
She just keeps on going, not counting the cost
And builds up her hair as she builds up her life
With elaborate care as the dutiful wife.
When her husband's away on some scheme of his own
She has friends everywhere and she's never alone.
And the Rover's Return is still run on oiled wheels
By a stylish landlady who knows how it feels
To be shabby and poor and rejected by all,
And she never forgets although now she walks tall.
So lift up your glasses and let's give a toast
To landlady Bet, hostess with the most,
Who still reigns supreme in her own special way,
And although I don't know her, she brightens my day.

Anne Treharne

Queen Sharon

Sharon's her name, she's cool and she's tough,
And sorts the men from the boys when the going gets rough,
She's fiery and fearsome and nobody's fool.
When the *Vic* is in trouble, she loses her cool.
Her past is the problem, it made her this way,
But it gives her the edge on a person who's grey.
With charisma and style, she tackles her life,
Each day in the pub where there's trouble and strife.
She takes on each worry as part of the trade,
And works hard at her job and the life she has made.
Some think of this lady as brassy and bold,
But when Nature made Sharon, it then broke the mould.
So you see why *Eastenders* just has to be seen,
On Tuesday and Thursday: it features a *Queen.*

Wilma Cunliffe

The Street

We tune in each week and we question,
Will Reg marry mousey Maureen,
Will Curly get the Manager's job,
Or is it only his dream.

Will mischievous Mike get his car back,
That devious Doug sold for a Merc,
Will Emily ever get over
The interfering of Pensioner Perce.

And what's this we see at *The Queen's*,
Liz's angry with her jealous Jim,
Will she end up back at *The Rover's*,
Or will Willmore allow him back in.

Will Ivy ever stop interfering,
Will Vera hold her venomous tongue,
Will Jack ever hit the jackpot,
Or will Ivy ever get back with Don.

Will Derek ever stop dithering,
Will Mavis regret marrying him,
Will Sally always be serious,
Will Raquel always be dim.

Will Bet be better off without Alec,
Will Ken cope with troublesome Trace,
Will Angie do well with her ambitions,
Will Deidrie need to find a new place.

We tune in each week in our millions,
It's not murderous, or violent or tough,
We must prefer kitchen-sink drama,
Cos it seems we just can't get enough.

Christine Lockton

Untitled

Arthur Fowler takes the biscuit,
In Albert Square he has to risk it,
He's playing away whilst remaining at home,
And the instant it rings he dives for the phone!
His wife's oblivious to his little affair,
Cos she's too busy moaning or flicking her hair.
He seems a lot happier with his bit on the side,
A woman with whom he's able to confide.
I wonder if they talk about gardening in bed,
Or maybe hoe-hoeing in the potting shed!
This could develop into a full length feature
But it's only a part, played by actor Bill Treacher.

Sheila Kennedy

My Pledge to Reg

Oh Reggie you're my hero
A supermarket star
Such style and poise like Poirot
Those looks have got you far.

Twinkling eyes - they tease me
Behind those spectacles,
When I watch you on the telly
I think I hear church bells.

Quick kiss behind the baked beans
Cuddles in the store,
A sexy wink amongst the greens,
Who could ask for more.

Let's float upon your water bed
Away into the night,
Never mind what Mavis said
We'd make a lovely sight.

So I'm going for an interview
To see my Reginald.
In his office just we two
To Bettabuys I'm sold.

B Hoskin

Alf Roberts

Alf Roberts is the grocer
Who keeps the Corner Shop;
He sells fresh milk and crusty bread
And lemonade and pop.
With fruit and veg and frozen food
He's always well supplied,
And in his white and pristine coat
He really takes such pride.
Though sometimes he looks worried
He has been known to smile
And with his friendly customers
He'll chat a little while.

He listens to their troubles
And helps them when he can
He tells them what they ought to do
He is that kind of man.
A pleasing personality, he is no raving beauty
When on the local council
He always did his duty.
But now he thinks the time has come
When he should take his ease
Together with wife, Audrey,
To do just as they please.
I could go on and write much more
But now it's time to stop.
Oh, Alf, how I shall miss you
When you leave the corner shop.

Josephine Stuart

Alf and Audrey

When you pull down the shutters and close the door
Remember, remember those days of yore,
When Renee passed on and you became,
A shopkeeper *on the street*, your claim to fame.

You worked, you slaved, by night and day,
Until eventually you made it pay,
Though many times you seemed so forlorn,
It was all worthwhile when *Alf's Mini Market* was born.

But all work and no play, made Alf a dull boy,
Until Audrey appeared and turned sorrow to joy,
And side by side they worked as a pair,
Which made competition easier to bear.

But now Father Time has had his say,
He's decided it's time they *call it a day*
They have found a buyer but who can tell
Whether *Alf's Mini Market* will do so well.

Now all we can say to our loveable couple,
Is wish them *Farewell* without any trouble,
The name of the game is do your own thing,
If you wish to come back just *give us a ring*.

M M Pattison

Bold and Brassy

Bold and brassy is *Our Ve*
She's always moaning but
as happy as can be.
She's got *our Tommy* and
our Jack, whatever Jack
does she always gives him flack.
A mother and a bit is our
Ve, she's had too many
hassles as far as I can see.
With *our Terry* and the
Law she's had more than
her fair share of it all.
On the front she's hard,
hard and steady, but really
inside she's as soft as a teddy.

She's had to be loud,
loud and outspoken because
if she wasn't she just
might end up broken.
She copes so well, so
well with it all it makes
me laugh each time I
hear her bawl; so come
on now let's give a cheer
to someone who inspires
us each and every year!

S Swindells

92

Roly-Poly

Such a shame about old Roly-Poly,
Why is it no-one seems to care?
But he does puff and huff
About all sorts of stuff
As he struggles to rise from his chair.

Why does nobody love Roly-Poly?
For the Woolpack's a great little earner,
Though he has a good try
He never knows why
They all say, 'No, Mr Turner.'

He's a gourmet is old Roly-Poly,
And he serves up the finest, the best,
Salmon without chips
Fruit without pips
And he frequently says, 'Be my guest.'

There's a strange thing about Roly-Poly,
He pretends he's incredibly straight,
So he'll always say sorry
If it fell from a lorry
And push the culprit straight through the gate.

Why do they all rag Roly-Poly?
Why make him pout and look hurt?
But they always will titter
Behind his best bitter
Then he gets all offended and curt.

So drink a toast to old Roly-Poly,
Let's shout it, not just a murmur,
As he eyes up the wenches
When he roughs it on benches
Let's hope one will say, 'Yes, Mr Turner!'

Evelyn Thomas

What's on TV Competition

They call her brassy,
and very sassy,
the toughest you've ever seen.
But look beyond
those curls so blonde
of the drinkers' favourite queen.
The glorious Bet -
the fiercest yet -
has a great big caring heart:
her brandy supplies
and words so wise
show she's mistress of her art.
With that cigarette,
she doesn't let
her customers start any bother:-
she'll clear them out
with a gentle shout
(sometimes she's just like their mother!)
Her crew at the back,
Betty, Raquel and Jack,
and the lately departed Liz
keep us all amused,
and the customers boozed -
behind the bar, it's showbiz!
Bet's known the ache
of her own heartbreak,
but she'll probably never learn.
Alec ran away
so now Bet can play,
but who knows - will her Rover return?

Teresa Gooch

94

Mandy Jordashe - Brookside

His brutal blow, sent me in a spin -
Why on earth, had I let him back in?
We'd found this *Haven* all we need -
Just like birds we had felt *set free*
From the cruel torture of the man I wed
Now he is back, a day I dreaded
My face is swollen, eyes bruised and black,
How could I go on, hiding the fact.
My daughter took my own pain away -
At breakfast, she lowered her head to say -
Daddy was cold, in bed last night,
So he asked me to hold him, close and tight!
The elder daughter stared at me!
'No Mum, please, it just can't be.'
We must do something, before it's too late
To go on, would mean, a certain fate
That was the way, it had to be.
Plans must be made, we'd wait and see
Crushed tablets in his drink were sought,
But, my daughter *Beth* and I were caught
He lurched across the room at me
Like a *madman*, I had no time to plea -
Then my child became the subject to attack,
I drove the knife, in her father's back,
We live in fear, should someone know,
He's buried deep, in the patio!

Rosemarie Woodhall

95

Ode to Mavis

Fluttery, fussy, prim and neat,
Mavis lives in Coronation Street.

Quivering, querulous, easily shocked,
She was surely *born* to be mocked!

Her narrow mind an open book,
Rita can slay her with a look!

Self-righteous and an awful prude,
Thinks most men coarse and rude;

Except her Derek, whom she adores,
(One of the Streets notorious bores);

But, despite Derek's pompous air,
They really are a devoted pair;

And the show would not be complete
If Mavis were to leave the Street.

We'd miss her woeful, wistful sighs,
The way she rolls those soulful eyes,

And when she bleats '*I don't reely know!*'
(Shaking her head, to and fro),

Laughter sweeps throughout our land -
Impersonators think she's grand!

Their favourite was Miss Bette Davis,
Now they're all mimicking Mavis!

So, Mavis dear, just stay as you are,
You may not be a Hollywood star,

But to us fans, you're *such* a treat,
You are, in fact, just up our Street!

Audrey Dennison Loach

The World's Handsomest Man

He sets the pulses racing,
Girls all sigh and swoon.
All eyes are soon upon him,
His presence fills the room.
Handsomer than Richard Gere,
Mel Gibson, Cruise and Costner.
He has something the rest all lack,
Deportment, style and posture.

He's debonair and elegant,
Not a thing can faze him.
Ladies kneel as if in church,
They venerate and praise him.
He's worshipped now throughout the land,
From Barnstaple to Perth.
You must know who this *sex-god* is,
That's right, it's - Reg Holdsworth -.

Stuart Carey

98

Ode to Curly Watts (Coronation Street)

Poor. old Curly,
What is it about you
That makes the girls neglect you
And makes you feel so blue?

Poor, old Curly,
Your hair so needs a comb,
Just as you need a loving wife
To brighten up your home.

Poor, old Curly,
You're the saddest man in town,
Since your old housemate, Angie,
Went off and let you down.

Poor, old Curly,
I though you'd found your mate;
But your fiancée, Kimberley,
Shared the selfsame fate.

Poor, old Curly,
Good luck at Bettabuys.
Here's hoping a bright future brings
An end to all your sighs.

F Wood

Lou Beale From Eastenders

She ruled the whole of Albert Square
While sitting on her derrière
She'd had three kids, during the war
Fighting off hunger from her door
She could combat all your fears
Or just as well reduce you to tears
With family problems she could cope
Then off to the Vic she'd slope
To sit and gossip with her mates
After clearing the dinner plates
'Old Arfur ain't got a lot on,'
She'd confide to Dot Cotton
New Zealand was home for her eldest son
But how he hated leaving his old Mum
Pete now ran the fruit and veg stall
Something learnt when he was small
Pauline had such a dreary life
But was a good mother and wife
Whoever she beckoned would come crawling
Knowing for sure they'd be in for a bawling
With a tongue as sharp as any knife
She never meant to cause such strife
She was a lady to be feared
She wouldn't let the Beale's be smeared
An iron lady it must be said
Long before Thatcher raised her head
She never had much sex appeal
Did our old friend Lou Beale
Pauline found her where she lay
The day the Angels took her away.

Denise Hodgkin

Street

There's Mavis Wilton on this show
With her Famous *I Don't Really Know*.
There's also Mike with his big cigar
A double Scotch and a big flashy car

There's Vera, Jack and Baby Tom
Ivy, Denise and Cabbie Don.
Andy, Steve, Liz and Jim
Sally, Rosie and Kevin

Rachel, Bet in the Rovers Return
Gail and Alma for egg and bacon.
Alf and Audrey for a loaf of bread
Will Curley and Angie end up In bed?

There's Rita Sullivan in the Kabin
Deidre Tracey and not forgetting Ken.

Emily, Phyllis and Percy love
They're all famous faces down at the pub.

They all live in a street we all know
And I'm sure there's a few that would like to go.
To see all the faces we see three times a week
There's only one like it Coronation Street.

Clifford Looker

Untitled

Jack Duckworth
Is the man in my life.
I'd love to be Vera
Who plays his wife.

He walks down the street
To the pub where he works.
He chats to his mates
In the cellar he shirks.

He's always in trouble
Never does anything right.
But I'd love to be with him
Anytime of the night.

I may be crazy
Or slightly barmy.
But the one I refer to
Is actor Bill Tarmey.

Janet Davis

Pat Phoenix Alias Elsie Tanner

She was the Prima Donna of the operas
You know the ones I mean.
To all of us, they are the soaps
The ones we see on the TV screen.

Her name of course was Elsie Tanner
The perfectionist of the Street.
It would be a difficult task to find
A more nicer person to meet.

She was the professional of the profession
Her perfection second to none.
But alas now our poor Elsie
Has departed, but memories linger on.

We will never forget our Elsie
As she fought to the very end.
Not just because of her acting
But because she was everybody's friend.

She won the hearts of millions
As she carried so high the banner.
And acted out the character
Of The Street's Elsie Tanner.

She will always be remembered
We will never forget her name.
She deserved all the accolades
That brought her loads of fame.

And so it's farewell to Elsie
The perfectionist to the very end.
But most of all - God Bless her
For being such a marvellous friend.

W J Cornford

Dot Cotton

Eastenders is a BBC soap, it's shown two nights a week,
And if you miss an episode, on Sundays it's repeat,
The area is Walford, the local is the Vic,
And from the market stalls be sure a bargain you can pick,
But when you go to Albert Square, you'll meet a special lady,
God fearing and good living too, although not quite a fairy,
Who can wave a magic wand and bring the world to rights,
But of her neighbours she sure knows their problems and their
                                                    plights,

Dot Cotton be the lady, her face is so well known,
A cigarette hangs from her mouth, this makes her look well worn,
Which isn't so surprising when you hear about her life,
Struggling through her younger years to be the perfect wife,
To Charlie, quite a chancer, now departed sad to say,
And their son whom they named Nick and devilish in his ways,
But no matter what he does or where he cares to roam,
There is a welcome on the mat when he returns home,
To earn a little extra cash, Dot works the launderette,
Willing to do someone's wash if they're not at their best,
She likes a little tipple too, tomato juice or sherry,
And after two or three or more, like Christmas she's quite merry,
But Dot was sad when Ethel, her friend moved from the square,
For memories of days long gone they often sat and shared,
But they keep in contact for friendship lingers on,
Like Ethels thoughts of *Willie* her pet dog sadly gone,
Yes Dot sure has a kindly heart, she's always there to help,
And when she has her aches and pains, she calls on Dr Legg,
But if in every street there was a good soul like dear Dot,
Everyone would have a friend, a gift that can't be bought.

Margaret Carr

Bet

First lady of the Rovers
Who would dare to say anything less
A dazzling smile as she pulls a pint
And a painted on leopard skin dress!
Now when hubby decided to leave,
Choosing life in the sun on a cruiser
She stuck out her chest, put on her lips,
There's no way Bet is a loser.
Come through to the back, she beckons
A pot of tea has always been brewed
The special is *Betty's Hot Pot*
You'll never go short of food . . .
A perfect hostess with the punters
Expression never sad
It's fine to be carefree, untroubled,
When your barman is *Jack the Lad*
Through the years we've seen her change
Seen her ups and downs on the street
But one things sure not to alter,
Our Bet is a hard act to beat!

Deborah Maxwell

Fowler Play

Oh Arthur you're stupid, incredibly dense,
I'd imagine at your age you'd have much more sense
than to have an affair behind Pauline's back
yet be highly indignant when she's on the same track.
Typical man, you just cannot see it,
trying to have your own cake and eat it.
Playing the lover, breaking the rule,
truly a coward playing the fool.

Make some decisions, sort out your life.
What do you want, a lover, or wife
who always stands by you but lacks the old fire.
Was it marriage to you that squashed her desire.
You can leave behind family and friends for Christine,
Albert Square will condemn you as heartless and mean.
Maybe you'll be happy and so glad you ran
but I suspect you'll end up a lonely old man.

Lorraine Jordison

Todd

The characters go and
The actors all change.
Some to play the same part
Even that isn't strange.
As the sig' tune begins, though
It does feel odd.
To be sat watching Neighbours
And know there's no Todd.

Though Kylie has long gone
There'll still be that scene.
Where Madge keeps in touch with
Her daughter Charlene.
And if Kylie decides
That she wants to repeat.
Former glories her role
Awaits in Ramsey Street.

But if Schmid does decide
He wants to be back in.
They will have to discover
That Todd had a twin.
But there's no chance for Todd
To return to the screen.
Unless like Bobby Ewing
It was all someone's dream.

Failing that then the best
That Neighbours can deliver.
Is a bit part as Todd's ghost
In poor Phoebe's mirror.

Paul Bush

Ethel

Remember Ethel Skinner, late of Albert Square?
A real endearing lady (although not quite all there)
Her conversations are a wonder, as the words come out all wrong
She loves a good old knees-up and a good old Cockney song.
A champion of the aged, and a thorn in the side for Dot.
A pensioner she might be, but she'll soon let you know what's what.
When dressed up for a party, she sometimes looks quite silly,
But I remember most, the cry, 'Have you seen my little Willy?'

Theresa Miles

108

Our Phyllis - Jill Summers

A lady who's seen many summers
Enjoying a *Gill* at the Rovers,
With a keen eye on Percy,
Who is there at her mercy,
Though he strongly resents her come-overs.

This talented actress of mirth
Still ignoring the date of her birth,
Once a slick station porter,
The acting bug caught her,
Now she plans to be salt of the earth.

When the *Glamour Grans* mounted the catwalk
Phyllis knew she had no time for that sort,
With her fresh violet rinse
She had soon made a clinch
And the Street's recognition she'd bought.

Many jobs have been hers in her time
Just revealing she's still in her prime,
Courting days still before her,
The viewers adore her,
For flirting suits Phyllis just fine!

Percy's treatment to her can't get worse,
And the message she gets in reverse,
She ignores his evasions
With friendly persusasions,
A fighter who never looks fierce
Our adorable dear - Phyllis Pearce.

Beatrice Johnson

Reflections

When Jack Duckworth looks in the mirror
        What do you think he sees?
Does he see a downtrodden barman
        The hen-pecked husband of V?

Does he wince at his sagging jawline
        And his features lacking in class?
Does he see just an all time loser
        With pockets empty of brass?

Or does he see in his reflection
        A vision of what he would be?
A man about town, a charmer,
        A gay dog ripe for a spree.

Does he wring his hands at the injustice
        That keeps him strapped for cash?
And that but for the want of spondulix
        He'd cut such a hell of a dash?

If Lady Luck would court him
        And give him one half of a chance,
He'd show the world what he's made of
        And give it a bonny dance.

But alas here lies the problem
        But alas here lies the rub,
He's only a down-at-heel barman
        In a Weatherfield backstreet pub.

Mavis Smith

As Seen on TV

I think TV is fabulous
It really is a treat
to settle down in front of it
For *Coronation Street*.

The Street is very dear to me
I've watched it from the start
The players whether fools or fine
are all close to my heart.

Reg Holdsworth is my favourite
With posturing bumbling gait
is waiting for his shop workers
to make sure they're not late.

An actor must have lots of skills
to make believe his role
Ken Morley (actor) he plays Reg
with all his heart and soul.

Reg the comic, Reg the fool
Reg will never break the rules.
Reg is honest, tells no lies
unless it suits him otherwise.
Reg the lover, Reg the rake
Reg the one you love or hate.
Mr Holdsworth is a bore
But Reg is a man you can't ignore.

Reg can be funny or sad
Downright stubborn or bad
But most of all for me
The very best upon TV.

Dorothy Perry

Ballad of Dot Cotton

Down in an East End Launderette,
There's a woman enjoying a cigarette.
She needs some tea cos her cough is rotten,
And she goes by the name of Dorothy Cotton.
She'll size you up with just one look,
Before she quotes from the Good Book.
Then she'll tell you about her poor son, Nick,
Who killed the landlord of *The Vic*.
Her good friend, Ethel's often silly,
Looking for her little Willy.
But, if you find yourself in a spot,
There's no one kinder than our Dot.
Young Nigel lodges with her still,
Though some say it's against his will.
He's often been known to tell a howler,
Which is more than can be said
For Pauline Fowler -
She's supposed to help Dot wash the clothes,
But some mornings would rather doze.
Still, the pair of them enjoy a good natter,
About things that don't really matter.
So if you want to know
Who's doing what to who,
Dot Cotton's the one who'll give you a clue.

Anthony Williams

Bet Plans Alec's Return

Word came from a Southampton pal,
That Alec had found a new gal.
Indeed she was slimmer,
And younger and trimmer,
A chanteuse by the name of Chantal!

The bar of the Rovers fell quiet,
Bet declared she would go on a diet.
Rising rage in her chest
Split her leopard skin vest
And near caused a Weatherfield riot!

Now Betty's hot-pot is a treat,
And respected the length of the street,
But the dish is too filling,
So Percy was willing
To lend Bet his recipe sheet.

It's a fact well known to be sure,
Percy served in the catering corp,
But his liver and onions
Gave poor Bet the runions -
So she weighed a lot less than before!

Now her appetite's that of a mouse,
But she gave Percy drinks on the house.
She said, 'Thanks Percy cock,
Now I'll fit in me frock,
And bring back that little fat louse!'

Caroline Shore

Mavis

Mavis you are prudish, shy and discreet
Do something wild, be the talk of the street,
Don't sit there sipping a glass of sweet sherry
Have a few gins get drunk and be merry.

Come on Mavis do something shocking
Wear silky black undies, suspenders and stocking
Be late for work or don't go at all.
Go out and have fun go AWOL.

Put on your makeup do your hair in curls
Go down the Rovers, have a drink with the girls
Derek won't mind he's a reasonable guy
If worse comes to worse you could tell him a lie.

Well I don't really know! I suppose you would say
So forget it Mavis, let's call it a day.
I know for certain you wouldn't give it a try
You'll always be prudish, discreet and shy.

Susan Briddick

Prisoner Cell Block H

I enter the prison
Each week on TV.
To watch Cell Block H
And good old Bea.
She has a rough
Caustic charm.
When inmates run riot
Bea stays cool and calm.
Old Vinegar Tits
Gets hopping mad.
Bea is the queen
Unruly and bad.
Bea is the top Dog
And over them all.
The prisoner's jump
When they hear Bea call.
Bea is in prison
For shooting her spouse.
He was a mongrel
A cad, a louse.
So in H Block now
Bea must serve her time.
Because the Judge said
She committed a crime.
I'm here each week
With Bea on TV.
Cos there but for the grace
Of God, goes me.

A Dean

A Night at the Opera?

A night at the opera is not to be missed
If you believe what the critics all say,
But there's a much better way of spending your time
Entertainment all night and all day.

In the comfort of your own home you can watch
Lots of programmes, you need never mope,
From music and comedy, films and cop shows
And for *Opera* there's our favourite soap.

Yes down on the street, there's a lot going on,
At Bettabuys and a small corner shop,
It's a good job Audrey at last made Alf see sense
Many more balm cakes, he would have gone pop.

For a warm friendly chat and a dish of hot pot
There's a welcome at a popular bar.
Though the odd scuffle mounts, Bet soon sorts it out
And it's back to enjoying a *jar*.

Egg and chips all day long can be had at Jim's cafe
Percy's favourite is a toasted teacake
Though it's Alma and Gail keeping the tea on the go
Mike Baldwin enjoys a cut of the stake.

With Kevin, he's got a good worker on cars
And a small printing business to hand.
But he's more famous for his fights with old Ken,
From the Rovers, he could well be banned.

But there's one more pair who without it would seem
Coronation Street would not be the same,
With all that Jack puts her through and son Terry too,
Vera Duckworth's life could not be called tame.

K Pinder

116

A Day Trip to the Coast

The fumble of hands for rough tunics, the groping of feet for scuffed
                                                                    boots,
Out into the heat of a desert, where the sun bleaches hair to the
                                                                    roots;
A bugle-blast of a morning, time to start feeding an army of men,
With their bear-like scratchings and rumbles, and grumbles of:
                                                        'Porridge again.'

No thanks from the ranks of soldiers, no praise from an officers'
                                                                    mess,
Just a round of noise from eating-irons, and the sound of
                                                        brave-hearted jests,
While they fling hard tack around the tent, despite his stern berating,
With laughing cries of, 'Blimey, Perce - we could use this as
                                                        armour-plating!'

These are the men of the Seventh Armoured, the legendary Desert
                                                                    Rats,
All here to fight - some here to die - are the warriors in soup-plate
                                                                    hats;
And Percy is ladling out porridge, with seconds for those who want
                                                                    more,
Tonight he'll be making them gravy - lifeblood of the Catering Corps.

A littlish man in enormous shorts, with legs all puffy and peeling,
(If T E Lawrence ever got sunburn, then P Sudgen knows the
                                                                    feeling)
But Percy is doing vital work - what's a Tommy without his pud?
And his have the heft of a sandbag - like a cookhouse pudding
                                                                    should.

The queue has started to whisper, newly cut orders are trickling
                                                                through:
'Bloody Hell! Across Devil's Gardens? Then them rumours they must
                                                        have been true,
It might be a bit bleedin' tricky, a push all the way to the sea -
I've written to the missus - if I don't make it, then post this for me.'

Percy took the letter in silence, while the rest gave a nervous cheer,
'If we don't get cooked in a 'brew-up' we'll see you back here for a
                                                                    beer!
We're feelin' a bit bleedin' restless - I'll enjoy a day trip to the
                                                            coast . . .'
Said with a grin and a tremble, it wasn't meant as some kind of
                                                                boast.

October 23rd in the Rover's, Percy's staring into his half-pint,
Boxed in by youngsters much taller, he's hard to see as some kind of
                                                                giant,
Dart players smirk and nudge at each other, 'He's lost down memory
                                                                lane!'
But Percy's inside a quiet mess tent - with the dead men who queue
                                                            there again.

So quiet it was in that mess tent - after the battle of El Alamein.

Murray Brough

118

Mercy, Percy!

Percy Sugden is the true gent of The Street,
For any young lady he'll give up his seat.
He did his bit for his country during the war,
Serving up spuds in the Catering Corps.
More lately he's given his time to the charity shop,
While Emily wished that at home he would stop.

Percy likes to get about and visit his old mates.
But using public transport is one thing he really hates.
Emily sometimes volunteers to take him for a spin,
But Percy's backseat driving really does her head in.
So she heads for The Rovers after each of their trips,
And downs several double sherries, with a packet of crisps.

When it comes to watching out for folk, Percy likes to take a stand,
As The Street's lone *Homewatch*, he thinks he's in command.
Some people take offence, but his intentions are all good.
It's not our hero's fault that he's misunderstood.
Like a real Desert Rat, he likes to *have a go*,
But people who don't know him well, call him *nosey so and so*!

Says Percy, 'If a job's worth doing, it's worth doing well.'
Put him in a uniform, and you can almost watch his head swell.
As a lollipop man, he sure had plenty of nerve.
He'd leap out from nowhere, and cause cars to swerve.
Drivers, to avoid him, took alternative routes,
And left Percy standing idle, in his hobnailed army boots.

In bad weather he'll don his cap and his scarf.
Then down to The Rovers to have a quick half.
Phyllis tries to tempt him with a warming hot toddy.
But everyone knows she's just after his body.
Yes, there's not many things give our Percy a scare.
But watch him retreat when he spots Phyllis' blue hair!

Ron Makin

Untitled

Angie was the Queen of the Vic
And Den he was her man
But now he is pushing up Daisies
While she's away getting a tan.

Arthur is having the time of his life
With his little secret affair
But it's curtains if anyone tells his wife,
'Cause he'll end up in intensive care.

Catherine McGuggon

Elsie Tanner

Elsie was more than a character,
She gave *Coronation Street* zip,
Whether she argued with Hilda
Or gave Annie Walker some lip.
Elsie was really Pat Pheonix,
And Pat, just like Elsie had style,
There won't be another like Elsie
In the *Rovers* for many a while.

M Holland

Joe Sugden

Joe and brother Jack were born on Emmerdale Farm,
Where life seems to me, to be anything but calm.
Their poor mother Annie tries to keep the brothers friends,
Row after row, she must be at her wits end.
Joe, being the younger of the two,
Was always trying to tell Jack what to do.
Joe's made many a mistake and been called a fool,
Unlike brother Jack who's as stubborn as a mule.
Joe's a ladies man and likes to have a fling,
Everyone's wondering, who's next to wear his ring.
Unlucky in love and married twice,
Do you think Lynn Whitley, will make it thrice.
Lynn's not so popular they call her a bitch,
But now old Bill's dead, they say she's very rich.
She's not all that bad, in fact she's kind at heart,
Annie's got a job keeping Joe and Lynn apart.
Joe's back on the farm after Frank gave him the boot,
Maybe it's true, he's after Lynn's loot.
What will Rachel feel when she hears the news in Leeds,
Where her step-father Joe's been sowing his seeds.
Rachel was the one Lynn's husband Pete really loved,
'Til her mum Kate, killed him and sent him to heaven above.
We wish Joe and his family, happiness in all that they do,
You've been on our screens so long, we feel as if we know you.

Sandra Shewan

Alma

With Alma's eyes so large and deep and dark,
A fanciful observer might surmise
That unfulfilled immortal longings spark,
And tragic forces flash in Alma's eyes.

Though once as Cleopatra, Egypt's queen,
She bathed in asses' milk to Carry On;
But Antony is vanished from the scene,
The purple sails of former glory gone.

Now serving chips and pies and washing plates,
A fan might think her story incomplete,
And wonder what new tragedy awaits
For Alma on the world's most famous Street.

Robert Marks

Reg Holdsworth

Reg Holdsworth is a bossy bloke
With all his supermarket folk
He's a creep with women he particularly likes
He thinks he's funny and really bright
When, to be honest, he'll find this sore
I think he is an utter bore.

He's stubby and fat with beady eyes
His wispy white hair not tried to disguise
Grows around his circular head
His face sticks out with cheeks bright red.

His dress sense, golly, why oh why?
His silky shirts and bright bow ties
His shiny glasses and shiny shoes
Could hit the headlines of tomorrow's news.

All in all he's not too bad
He talks quite posh
But he's not gone mad
Reg Holdsworth is a real nice bloke
Coronation Street's standing joke.

Emma Wey (11)

124

Vera

Vera, our Vera,
Coronation Street Diva,
A curious mixture, no doubt.
She's loudmouthed and coarse
quick to anger; gale force,
Whenever us Duckworth's lose out.
If you threaten our Jack
She'll give you a wack
then turn round and give him a clout.
Vera's a mother,
with love like no other,
Our Terry's a good boy, she sighs,
It's those lot that's done this
that Lisa, that Dennis,
even Ivy's been spreading her lies,
but look at our Tommy,
love him; so bonny,
I'll have to leave Betta Buys.
Our Vera Duckworth
So salty, so stalwart,
Bright curly wig; brassy and vain.
She'll champion a friend
and fight to the end,
in spite of our Jack's restrain.
Yet loved ones desert her
and life's setbacks hurt her
she'll get up and fight on again.

Dorothy Berni

Poor Old Arthur

You've got to admire him, he's got a lot to bear,
Married to drab old Pauline, living in Albert Square.
His children Mark and Martin not forgetting poor Meechelle
Always have a problem, always something to tell.
His gardening contracts finished he hasn't got a job.
Next news he'll be borrowing from the heavy mob.
He'll hide himself away again perhaps go off his head
Spending too much time alone, in his little shed
But soon he'll be on top again, I'll tell you what will do it,
A quiet secret meeting with Mrs Christine Hewitt.
You really can't begrudge him his little bit of pleasure
Good luck Arthur Fowler, you cuddly little treasure.

V France

126

Untitled

On meeting Reg Holdsworth, a gent with clarity of vision
One is immediately tempted to make a certain incision
His insular actions and school of thought
Provide him with joy at the goods you have bought.

He chases the ladies at a rare old pace
Confident supreme that he is winning the chase
The ladies involved feel he is cheeky to try
And on failing Reg goes back to beloved Betta Buy.

The girl of his dreams works at the store
Reg's incessant chase continues once more
He proclaimed his love as she worked in the aisles
With peacock-like strut, working his wiles.

His offer he chopped to purchase Alf's store
But Alf and Audrey showed him the door   .
Reg whined and whinged and went round the bend
For he'd lost the shop to Brendan his friend.

Curly had little time to warm the seat of his chair
Before Reg was back with all his old flair
Reg is not the man to reason why
But he knew he'd lost a better buy.

P T Lynch

Reg

There's a man named Holdsworth - Reg,
Who does more than sell meat and two veg'.
He's a man of honour and pride,
(With a leer that's about ten foot wide).
Eyes of steely blue,
(That fix on to women like glue).

He's funny and witty - tells many a ditty
Down at the Rovers Return.
Impeccably dressed
With an air to impress,
What young girl's heart wouldn't yearn?

Maureen - his intended,
Thinks he's perfectly splendid
Which is more than her mother's impression.
She's constantly moaning,
Grumbling and groaning,
And says he's her cause of depression.

But for all his odd ways
What dullest days,
Without his bright sunny smiles.
So next time you see him,
Smile and greet him -
Resist that urge to run miles!

B J Ellis-Macey

Isabel Blair-Morgan

To pick up your pension, or just buy a stamp
load up with groceries, or more
if in Glendarroch, to manage it all
visit Isabel, at *Blair's Store*.

Charming and friendly, she'll put you at ease
a person well thought of by all
although very busy, she always finds time
for her friends and her work, in the Rural.

Enjoys a good blether and a really good laugh
though to sorrow, a stranger she's not
for grief has come often in Isabel's life
coping with it she's strengthened a lot.

Her husband in prison, she carried the load
of the guilt and the tragedy caused.
she brought up her son, ran the store and her home,
with a dignity, second to none.

Fatal loss of her son and her marriage dissolved
then an illness, everyone fears
she survived, fell in love and married again
this time hopefully, with less tears.

I M Elliott

129

Ten Minutes in the Life of a Bettabuys Manager

Careering past
The checkout tills
Looking pink
Around the gills.
The balding pate
With grey-edged trim
Flashes past
The baked bean tins.
Rumbled again
Another plot fails
Whilst in his wake
His jacket trails.
Then suddenly,
His piercing glare
Descends upon
A damsel fair.
'Maureen my love
Where have you been?
A lovelier smile
I've yet to see.'
Then instantly,
Above his chin
From ear to ear
A lecherous grin.
He's a likeable rogue
Some women dread
Especially when armed
With a water bed.

D J Purrington

RIP Dirty Den

There aren't many men
like Dirty Den
they're few and far between
the King of the Vic
knew many tricks
and most of them were mean.
Can Sharon be blamed?
or can she claim
her awful luck with men
isn't because she's doing it wrong
but because her dad was Den.
His wife, the beautiful Angie
turned to the bottle again
for her it was just like medicine
she drank to relieve the pain
His pals were from the underworld
shady characters all
when Den became involved with them
he was heading for a fall
I bet he thought he'd never
finish up in the river
not swimming, not even afloat
I bet he thought he'd never
even go near the river
unless he was in a boat
still he wasn't all bad
and my wife's quite sad
that we won't see him again
so this much I will wish you
Rest In Peace Dirty Den.

John Hurley

An Ode to Reg Holdsworth

Curly has to put up with you,
Rita does too,
But the people near the TV screen,
Can't help but laugh at you.

You really crack me mum up,
Me auntie and me dad.
They can't wait 'til the day
You'll be on a Bettabuy's Ad.

You're the cream of all store managers
(Or so me mum says)
And I hope they'll never be times
When there are no Reggie days.

If there comes a time for you to leave,
Just you remember this,
No-one can replace you Reggie lad,
You will be sadly missed.

Lynsey Spence (12)

Coronation Street

Coronation Street is the best
Bet is great, and so are the rest.
There down to earth just like reality
And true to life just like it should be.
There's the nice young couple Kevin and Sally
Then there's Reg who acts a bit do-lally
And there's Deirdre down on her luck with love
And the corner shop where Ken lives in the flat above.
And Curly, New Manager of Bettabuys
A bit of a dim-wit, but he's really quite nice.
And it wouldn't be the same without Vera and Jack
I hope they don't leave or get the sack.
It's three times a week we see the Street
When it comes on, out comes the stool and up go my feet.

Gloria Simmonds

Ode to Marcus Tandy

He wasn't really a nice man,
There's simply nothing to endear
Marcus Tandy to our hearts.
He's King Rat of the year.
He seemed to spend all his time
On the wrong side of the Law,
He was brutal and sadistic.
What was it in him I saw?
When it came to seducing a young girl
He didn't flinch to use his charms,
When it came to getting his own way
He didn't quail at bearing arms.
He would even stitch up his friends
If it meant he'd achieve his aims.
Never did he seem to tire
Of playing dangerous games.
I simply hated that awful programme,
Espana's El Dorado.
It was plagued with wooden acting,
And full of bluster and bravado.
And you can ask if t'was so bad why did I watch the show,
And I'll tell you I was forced to
By Marcus Tandy don't you know.
I really like that character
He was the best thing on the box.
For me he brought the show alive
The cunning wily fox.
In real life I wouldn't like him
But to the show he was heaven sent,
And it really made me sad indeed
When Marcus Tandy went.
So I hope the beeb will read this
And will say exactly when
Marcus, and El Dorado
Will be on our screens again.

S Watson

The Ballad of Maureen and Reg

He eyed his domain through bottle-thick lens,
That disguised his aquiline eyes.
That hovered above the cat-like grin,
As a predator patrolling his private skies.
And then he spied his timid prey.
Between the fish and the frozen pies,
So down swooped our hunter
The hawk of Bettabuys

She was scurrying down the aisle
Oblivious to what fate had planned.
When out popped a pouting, pale face
'Vous Permettez' it said; then kissed her hand.
'Oh,' cooed she, at his poetry
(You know what old romantics are)
As he captured her with Byronic lines
And a certain je ne sais quoi.

And now, of his conquest, he boasts aloud
With a heart almost fit to burst.
Of how none can resist his fatal charm
(Unless they see him coming first)
But always within a smiling distance,
Be it in the *Street* or in the store,
Walks the not-so-timid creature
The mouse that made the lion roar.

Kenneth Horsepool

135

Missing You

I don't have to think about it
For her image is plain as can be,
Who else but this certain person
Could make me say, 'That's just like me?'
How I wish she was back again with us,
Coronation Street isn't the same,
I think that by now you'll have guessed it
Oh! yes Hilda Ogden's her name.

Betty Squire

136

Emmerdale Farm

Set in a countryside that's full of charm
Here is a story of Emmerdale Farm
You could start with dear Annie
The Queen of the Dales
And there's Eric Pollard
Who's in charge of the sales.
Up on the farm there's Sarah and Jack
Wondering if Joe will ever come back
You could visit the Fish Farm and sample the trout
Where you'll find Mrs Pollard round and about
Up at the manor there's Frank and there's Zoe
And Nick the gardener raring to go
As you go through the village and walk past the shop
You see Kim on her horse going clipperty clop
Then it's into the Woolpack a nice local inn
Where you're greeted by Carol with an inquisitive grin
You see Alan Turner the landlord of the pub
Not forgetting Lynn Whitely in charge of the grub
There's gamekeeper Seth who looks after the land
And can often be found with a pint in his hand
Go spend a few days at the Holiday Park
Where sometimes you'll find Rachel and Mark
There's Archie the baby-sitter and Kathy and Chris
Who have not always found matrimonial bliss
So these are the people who should do you no harm
When working on stories about Emmerdale Farm.

Campbell Bannerman

Bev From Brookside

Twenty years washed away
as though they didn't exist
all because of an older man
whom you couldn't resist.
Your sister you've offended
you've shamed the family name
Bev, you must stop now,
playing this evil game.
If you continue
No friends you will keep
they're calling you *homewrecker*
trouble - you're in deep.
DD's very ill now
a convent, she is staying
and for her deceitful husband
to God she is praying.
Advantage you are taking
always asking for money
he's even brought your flat
the joke's no longer funny
So leave Ron alone
go back to where you came
give his wife and kids a chance
to have him back again.

Tammy Smith

Just Up Our Street

Oh Bet we love those earrings
And your flaunting, cheeky smile.
False eyelashes, long blond curls,
An' a cleavage *half a mile*

Designer frocks an' suits an' things
Flash jewellery everywhere.
The pay must be good at *The Rovers* -
No wonder you stay there!

Since hubby Alec departed
To Southampton by-the-sea,
It's like old times at *The Rovers*
With Bet back as Queen Bee!

Cunning, but every-bit loveable Jack,
With spectacles *still on the mend!*
Dotty Raquel providing the *glam*
And Bet Turpin - everyone's friend.

Mavis and Derek, Audrey and Alf,
Poor Curly - all on his own,
All of them eating tons of hot pot
Is it the only recipe known?

The trendy gear worn by Angie,
Who has no luck at all with her men!
Wonder if Deidre will ever get round
To making it up with Ken.

One day Bet will have to retire
'Though hopefully, not for years yet.
But whoever they put in *The Rovers Return* -
It won't be the same without Bet!

Val Hall

139

How do You Get Rid of Helen Daniels

How do you get rid of Helen Daniels?
I'd really like to know
She has been mugged, burgled and jilted
But still always on the go!

How do you get rid of Helen Daniels?
She must have nine lives
She has been kidnapped, fallen down stairs and had a stroke
I don't know how she survives.

Alexa Hart (12)

Bet Gilroy

Serene as any ocean liner lit
from painted bow to fashionable stern,
she sails her narrow course behind the bar
and greets each well-known rover's safe return.

She squares her shoulder pads and pats her hair,
advancing through the tidal flow of chat,
a classic figure-head, firm cleavage thrust
where gossip sprays the dregs of this and that.

She joins the verbal banter, razor-tongued,
while pulling pints and serving like a queen
bedecked with jewels, flamboyant dress too tight,
her ready smile less certain than it seems.

Behind the lipstick and that worldly air
of knowing all that fickle fate can fling,
she hides her disillusion and her scars
but fears the mask is slowly wearing thin.

She buys another frock - a bright disguise
to camouflage the signs she's getting old -
she gilds the fading lily but remains
a brassy barmaid with a heart of gold.

At closing time she bolts the public door,
counts the takings, hears the cold wind moan
and welcomes darkness like a faithful friend:
she dreams of love but spends the night alone.

Jean M Thomas

Ode to P P

C oarse of voice and blue of hair,
O utrageous flirt of ageing years,
R ound of hip and short of height
O utspoken critic of near and far
N evertheless, with heart of gold
A doring Des, she cooks and cleans,
T roubles not the hours she slaves,
I ndustrious woman: wanting work,
O ffering her services to one and all,
N eeding employment to fill her hours.

S he's been a widow for many a year,
T rue love and compassion she misses.
R etreating to *The Rovers* for a half
E avesdrops on others' business;
E nlightened then, she spreads the word,
T ongue - wagging pensioner of our time,
S avouring the snippets of gossip.

P ompous Percy she adores:
H ope springs eternal in her breast,
Y et unrequited is her love.
L ove-sick for his amorous glances,
L ong-suffering lady of the Street,
I mmune to sarcasm, soldiers on,
S ure Sugden will respond one day.

P ercy, her love, rejects ignores
E very advance she makes to him
A nd puts her down with scornful words.
R egardless, she, thick-skinned and hopeful,
C herishes thoughts of what's to come,
E ngrossed in dreams of future happiness.

Sandra E Coombs

142

Reg and Maureen

Reggie Holdsworth, lost his bid for the shop,
His attempt to seduce Maureen, was also a flop.

His unbridled passion, on his large water bed,
sent water cascading, over Derek Wilton's head.

Derek's bright idea, to fix the light to the ceiling
Left the store-room awash and Mavis reeling.

Maureen's mother, dislikes our Reg,
She tries to postpone the oncoming marriage.

Reg, is the *Proverbial* man about town
Always wearing a smile and never a frown.

The only thing that makes him stare.
Is the *prospective* mother-in-law, in her electric wheel chair.

His pulse rate goes up, beads of sweat on his brow
I wish she'd get lost, the interfering old . . .

Maureen's house is for sale, a buyer gets in touch.
As usual, her Mother, doesn't like him much.

The man's easy put off, buy her mother's antics
But as ever, our Reggie's, saved a few tricks.

He wants his Maureen, but not her Mother.
To share his life without any bother.

Not to be pestered from morning 'til dusk
To get rid of the dragon is definitely a must.

I've got a new position, and soon a new wife.
They'll do nicely, for the rest of my life.

Colin Mills

Jack the Lad

He works in the Rovers, he lives in the Street
His expression's a mixture of hope and defeat
With his green plastic pinny, his specs stuck with plaster
He looks like a joke, while his life's a disaster
But Jack's not downhearted, depressed or dejected
'Cause life's only given him what he expected
He's one of life's losers, a sponger, a skiver
But in spite of it all, our Jack's a survivor
He's content with his paper, his pint and a fag,
And the odd fiver *borrowed* from Vera's bag
To spend in the bookies, and all on one horse -
Another *dead-cert* - which loses of course
He's dogged by bad judgement, bad luck, a bad back
And a wife on the warpath - that's life for our Jack!

Kerry Tyrer

Raquel

This little story I'm going to tell
is about a barmaid called Raquel
what a beauty standing there
big blue eyes and golden hair.

She plays a part that's oh so funny
makes a dull night bright and sunny
Monday, Wednesday and Friday are such a treat
when we all go down the street.

Reg could not believe his eyes
When she resigned from Better Buys
Curly didn't stand a chance
when he took her to the dance.

She was a model long ago
but London didn't want to know
Came back home down in the dumps
then Des Barnes came up trumps.

She stayed with Des but not for long
Steph came home and she was gone
She thought she'd found her one and all
his name was Wayne *Mr Football*.

But he was a two timing fool
Raquel pushed him in the pool
So back to the Rovers she did go
broken hearted and full of woe.

She's supposed to be thick and not too bright
but she learned the rules of cricket over night
now she's on a sticky wicket
going out with Mr Cricket.

Terry Robinson

145

Reg Holdsworth - Heartbreaker

I lived for Coronation Street three times a week
To see my one and only love: suave and smiling.
Your cute round face brightened up my life.
How will I ever cope when you make *her* your wife?

Oh Reg, you've broken my heart;
You're in love with Maureen now.
I had my plans amidst the meat and veg,
But you'll never have the pleasure now, will you Reg?
You set my heart thumping with images of us in your water bed
But now I'm left sad and lonely, dreams adrift:
Goodbye Reg!

Jacquie Kelly

Curly Watts

Upon his head there's not a curl
Though Curly is his name.
He never seems to get the girl
But always gets the blame.

When first he came to Bettabuys
There didn't seem much future.
Stacking tins and checking pies
Then teaching Reg computer.

With granny specs perched on his nose
At Angela he peers.
His love for her that blooms and grows
Is not returned he fears.

He's had some girl friends in his time
One was very faddy.
She almost hooked him with her line -
'Mummy's asking Daddy.'

Star gazing through his telescope
Though Angie is his star.
He feels the future holds more hope
And hopes it won't be far.

His telescope is focused wide
Upon the window ledge.
But whose the one whose at his side?
Not Angie girl but Reg!

But now he's boss of Betta buys
It's really made his day.
Prap's now I'll get the girl he sighs
With Watts there is a way.

Edna Frances Little

A Safe Bet

Bet Lynch as was - Gilroy now,
The Rover's Return's sacred cow.

A post-menopausal Barbie doll,
An effervescent drinker's moll,
Poured into alarmingly revealing dresses,
With a face that's framed by platinum tresses.

She's busty and trusty - full of learning curves
Not always getting the breaks she deserves.

A statuesque lighthouse amidst the rocks,
Shining her light on the Street's beery flocks.
Soft as putty, hard as nails,
She keeps the lot on the rails.

The men in her life are merely asides -
Love is best left to the other brides.

To this Queen of the soaps I want to bow -
To pay homage to the Street's sacred cow.
Here's to you Bet, long may you reign.
Long live the Queen, again and again.

Kay Prout

148

Bad Neighbours

I've decided to stop watching Neighbours
And the reason's not hard to detect,
For it seems very odd
From Big Jim to young Todd
They all have the same bad defect.

They lie with such ease and abandon
It's like falling, to them, off a log.
The only one in it
I'd trust for a minute
Is the one they call Bouncer - the dog!

Madge lies to her husband, Paul cheats on his wife,
It really is no great surprise
That the young ones like Toby
And Phoebe, and Cody
Are soon making their own packs of lies.

I dread to think what this is doing
To the youngsters who watch day by day.
It's really a crime
That time after time
Those wrongdoers get their own way.

They now have a new generation
(For several years have gone by)
And his father, Paul
Will be proudest of all
When young Andrew tells his first lie.

I'm glad they're far off in Australia, and not living here in my town,
The Ramsay Street folk
Are no longer a joke
And their antics are getting me down.

Anna Ross Shearer

149

A Star

Johnny Briggs is a sort of ordinary name
But by being Mike Baldwin has brought him great fame,
A star in Granada's own Coronation Street,
And as a macho guy he is cast,
But when he smiles
His face transforms
Into a kind of loving person,
And with many others this poet is a fan.

Alma his lovely wife Mike really loves her,
Although he has caused her many a tear,
Mark his son is precious too
Born by an ex wife years ago,
An idea now it's by the way
Following a script for three to play,
Mike's young brother is to wed
So off to London it is read.

Mike, Mark and Alma have the time to spare
So they are going on a holiday
First the wedding fashionable exciting
These three are thoroughly enjoying,
Then they have such fun in London Town
The shows the places alas the time has flown.
So back to Coronation Street
Where old friends smile and greet.

Dorothy Fone

Pauline Fowler

Life is for ever up and down
For poor hard up Pauline Fowler
Living in a small part of town
Full of council houses, flats and towers.

Working hard to do her share
Trying to cope as a mum and wife
She experiences life being so unfair
Little happiness with a lot of strife.

But she is a woman so strong
The backbone to all her family
And it doesn't matter how long
She'll survive every day realities.

Pauline looks for an escape
But she's in such demand always
She's ready to give more than take
And her dreams fade in so many ways.

Her tired blue eyes show the pressure
Her attempts to keep herself going
Is one long struggle with little leisure
She's a homely woman, cooking, cleaning and sewing.

C Diamond

Toby Mangle

This is a poem about Toby Mangle
Who once got in a tangle
His problem was
He couldn't draw an angle.

Bouncer was his favourite dog
He once took him for a jog
While he took him for a walk
He met his friend and started to talk.

'What's the matter,' said his friend
'everything it doesn't end.'
So his friend told him to sit
And then taught him how to do it.

And now Toby Mangle
Won't get in a tangle
With his angles.

K Jones (10)

Goodbye to Dot Cotton

Poor old Dot Cotton was often forgotten
By family and friends in the square,
Poor Old Dot Cotton had a son who was rotten
Of his person you had to beware
Poor Old Dot Cotton's Charlie was trodden
By a lorry driven without due care
Poor Old Dot Cotton worked in the launderette quite often
With Pauline sometimes taking her fair share
Poor Old Dot Cotton's lodger Nigel was begotten
They made a peculiar pair
Poor Old Dot Cotton had a rather large bottom
And grey rampaging through her hair.
Poor Old Dot Cotton will soon be forgotten
By the viewers that sit in a chair
Poor Old Dot Cotton there's no need to defect to Hotten
Because the cast and the public still care!

C L Bickford

153

Sharon, Grant and Phil Too

Grant he fancied sexy Sharon
And soon he had her wed
But her gaze was soon to fall upon
His brother Phil instead

Fed up with Grant and his moody ways
She thought she'd seen the light
Her marriage was in numbered days
Now Phil was in her sight

Landing in the local jail
Grant had lost the head
Phil didn't pay his brother's bail
But took his place in bed

Now Grant was out of harm's way
Under lock and key
But he came back another day
Once they'd set him free

Sharon saw a turn about
She had a change of heart
Grant had changed without a doubt
So why were they apart

She made a vow, no more deceit
Give Grant another chance
And so the circle is complete
In this fairy tale romance.

I Findlay

154

Better Luck Norman!

Dame Fortune rarely smiles on Norman Watts,
  Dubbed *Curly*, as his hair is straight and lank!
His Lines of Love and Life are thick with knots!

His heart is scarred with Cupid's arrow shots;
  The love-boat Curly launched with Shirley sank.
Dame Fortune rarely smiles on Norman Watts.

He lost Raquel. He's now expending lots
  Of angst for Angie, so far drawing blank.
His Lines of Love and Life are thick with knots!

At Bettabuys, beset by crooks and clots
  There's always someone causing hanky-pank!
Dame Fortune rarely smiles on Norman Watts.

He's been a dupe of Holdsworth's and of Scott's -
  Less devious than either mountebank.
His Lines of Love and Life are thick with knots!

A manager at last! May future plots
  See Curly blessed in love as raised in rank!
Dame Fortune rarely smiles on Norman Watts, -
His Lines of Love and Life are thick with knots.

Marguerite Kendrick

The Hills are Alive

Fond memories we all have
Of the lady in the Street
Who worked so hard in the Rovers
Just to make ends meet

The familiar curlers and apron
And her singing voice so high
She loved a bit of gossip
But could never tell a lie.

She gave us many smiles
With her funny little ways
And who can forget the *muriel*
That stayed for so many days.

A good and honest person
So loyal to her man
He wasn't the best, but she loved him
And missed him so much - dear Stan.

They had a few lodgers through the years
Remember big Eddie Yates
She was like a mum to him
Well, it helped to pay the rates.

Since Hilda Ogden left
Who cleans the Rovers now?
I don't think it could be Jack Duckworth
'Cause he definitely wouldn't know how.

You were a little gem
Dear Hilda *or Mrs O*
No-one hears from you now
We were so sorry to see you go.

V Carter

156

Lament for Hilda Ogden

She lived in the Street did Our Hilda,
She was common, but loveable too;
Her curlers she wore 'neath a turban,
And mostly her pinny was blue!
She was't cleaner along down the Rovers
For Annie and later for Bet,
And she did for a doctor in best part of town,
Which she didn't let no-one forget!
Stan was the name of her husband,
And she stuck to him through thick and thin,
Though she nagged him she really did love him;
And she kept their house like a new pin!
Her great pride and joy in the kitchen
Was the *Muriel* painted on't wall
And the plaster ducks flying across it,
(One wouldn't stay upright at all)!
When Stan died poor Hilda was shattered
But she put on a dignified face.
When another chap wanted to wed her
She *couldn't* put him in Stan's place.

The Doctor's time came to retire,
His wife asked Our Hilda to pack.
They were both beaten up by some robbers;
The wife died, and things did look black.
The Doctor said, 'Please come and housekeep,
I do feel so bereft and so numb.'
Wi'out thinking she'd rise in the world now
Our Hilda said, 'Yes doc, I'll come.'

Bet gave her a party and laid on Champagne
Then she left. But without her the Street's not the same!

Wendy A F Martyn

Raquel

Raquel is a barmaid
Who models now and then
She wears the latest fashions
But she has no luck with men.

At first she dated Curly
That match was not to be
Although she was Miss Betterbuys
He fell for Kimberley.

Then along came Desmond Barnes
Who was good at spinning yarns
Though in the end Raquel could see
He preferred his ex-wife Stephanie

Wonderboy Wayne then came along
He had football on his mind
Unfortunately for Raquel though
He was not the faithful kind.

Let's hope now Raquel feels
Fed up of being used
And keeps a hold of Gordon
Even though he's no Tom Cruise.

He takes her to watch cricket
So in the end he'll show her
That by treating someone nice
You can bowl a maiden over.

Maxine Galloway

To Nick

Behind the Bar pulling pints,
Wicksey was seen most every night.
To roll his eyes at every girl,
where minds in turn became a whirl.

To love and leave became his motto,
'til Cindy hooked this handsome Romeo.
No more to flirt, or roll his eyes,
Our Cindy cut him down to size.

But Romeo's don't stay down for long
he left to sing another song,
And now in uniform he walks the beat,
to catch all those who sin and cheat.

For now our Nick has changed his ways,
singing songs of love will surely pay.
Today his heart beats just for one,
so for her he sings his song.

Hazel Lancaster

159

Beady Eyes and Woolly Cap

There's no mistaking this 'ere chap,
'Specially in his woolly cap,
Those beady eyes and long moustache
His dialect is far from posh.

The Woolpack is his favourite place
Sneaks off from work there, what a disgrace!
Always ready for a free pint or more,
Never seen drunk though, of that I'm sure.

He's dog and bike that's all he has
Since Meg has died, his wife his lass.
There's no-one to compare, he really is unique,
Without him Emmerdale, just wouldn't be complete.

Yes, Seth the chap, if you haven't guessed yet,
A special character you couldn't forget
There's only one thing left to say,
We hope in Emmerdale he will remain.

V A Wright

Hilda

Oh! How I miss *Hilda*
The Street's not the same
Curlers an' all
She was my favourite dame!
I wish she'd return to do all the chores
We don't see anyone *now* doing the floors!
The Rovers just sparkled when Hilda was there
And her and Stan, made such a good pair!
They all knew her tongue
Was worse than her bite
Although she never liked missing a fight!
So please bring her back - for a visit - or two!
Back to our screens - it would be a coup!

Paula Daniels

161

Street Wise Guy

There he struts along the street
With his nose held in the air.
Although Alf's shop now won't be his,
He simply doesn't care!

So now that promotion's his
And to Maureen he'll get wed,
Alas! catastrophe has struck
With his burst water bed.

Well, with those trendy blue specs
That just emphasise his eyes,
He would hardly be unnoticed
When he's in Bettabuys.

Poor Curly's just his scapegoat.
Now would this man sink so low?
There are many folk dislike him,
And Angie's one more foe.

It is really possible
That he looked like that from birth?
You know the man I speak of,
The Street's own Reg Holdsworth.

C Jeffries

162

Ode to Ena Sharples

Coronation Street is the name
Where Ena Sharples found her fame
She fought and worked hard all her life
And put up with a lot of strife
A battle was never far away
When good old Ena had her say.

Minnie Caldwell and Martha too
Joined her for their favourite brew
In the Rover's snug each day
Where they passed their time away
Their daily gossip and Ena's moan
Often made Annie Walker Groan.

Elsie Tanner was in the street
And for gossip, she was a treat
Elsie had a colourful life
But could never make a model wife
Ena rubbed her hands with glee
With every scandal from Elsie.

When Elsie left the street at last
Poor Ena's fun was almost passed
If they were still living in the street
They'd have Percy Sugden on his feet
What battles they would have together
They really would fight hell for leather.

Ena is now dead and gone
But still her memory lingers on
Although our Vera tries her best
The battle-axe crown she cannot wrest.

Rosemarie Edwards

Stardusted

Perchance to dream, perhaps to meet
One's favour characters from the *street*
Take's me shopping for fruit and veg,
To Bettabuys to see dear Reg.
Where overcome with mixed emotion
I merely wish him more promotion.
Then, leaving Reg, it's still quite early
I trot along to find our Curly.
And ask with not the least pretensions,
Regarding his plans, and future intentions.
But it's not just Curly and Reg and Co
That keep me viewing, this I know.
But all of the cast of a wonderful story
Who cover themselves in fame and glory.

Evelyn May Wardle

Reg Holdsworth

'Good morning Mr Watts
I trust you are quite well.
I'm leaving you in charge
For a meeting at half twelve.'

'Oh come off it Reggie,
You cannot fool me
You're going to see Mrs Naylor
It is so plain to see.'

'She has just changed her break
To twelve o'clock 'til one
You must think I'm daft
You're off to have some fun.'

'Now Mr Watts please
You must keep your voice down.
It's not at all like that
I have a meeting in town.'

'I don't believe a word
But then there's not much I can do.'
'You're quite right Mr Watts
So I'll say good day to you.'

Mark Tuckey

Jack Duckworth

We see you serving at the bar or cleaning out the cellar,
Stacking crates or bottling up - a very useful fellow.

Poor old Jack with all his bets forever losing out
What will he do when he gets home and Vera starts to shout?

Jack Duckworth, Jacko, to his mates chatting up the barmaids -
They are having none of it as he doesn't make the grade.

Raquel and Bet, Betty and Vera constantly plague his life
Poor old Jack give him peace and quiet and avoid his battle-axe wife.

Newton and Ridley, the brewery owners, wonder why he's there -
But as Bet knows, he comes in handy to give the rowdies a scare.

The Rovers Return would not be the same without old loveable Jack
Behind the bar, giving us a wink makes up for the things he lacks.

Well done Jack have a drink on me a pint of your very best,
Over the years you've stayed the pace and definitely passed the test.

Hilary J Murphy

A Pop at Pippa

How do you do it Pippa? Could I achieve it too?
I would like for just one day, to be as good as you.

Your house is always tidy, not a toy out of place,
When I've watched you on TV, I squirm in disgrace.

Your hanging out your washing, keeping caravans clean,
Giving good advice to everyone, and cooking in between!

You do it all in half an hour, whilst I in a day,
Run around in circles, I feel quite ashamed to say!

And whilst we're on the subject, you always look good too,
Does not your little boy, ever throw his lunch at you?

My children don't do this often, but you must know what I mean,
My face is still in my makeup bag, even though I'm clean.

I could never match all you do, and I could never be as fast,
Well the only way I know of, would be to join the cast!.

Dawn Galbally

Reg Holdsworth

I am a jolly plump Romeo
Who's name is Randy Reg
I'm often seen at Bettabuys
Lurking in around the veg.

I have chased a lot of women
A view of marriage in mind
Most of them just turn away
Saying Reggie, 'Do you think I'm blind.'

But now I've found my perfect lass
Miss Naylor's the one for me
Our love shall be eternal
And this you all shall see.

Now working life has took a turn
And my job was on the line
But now it's *Area Manager* Reg
And this title suits me fine.

My suffering assistant Curly Watts
He wished me all the best
Goodbye, good luck, good riddance,
To the Coronation Street pest!.

Ian Rodman

Bet

Bet is the name we've all come to learn
That we all think of at the Rovers Return,
Her suits come in colours of red, white or black,
And her one nagging pain is her cellarman Jack.
We've seen her in scenes where she's often quite sad,
Like the time when Victoria lost her Mum and her Dad.
Alec is the name of the man in her life
But just at the moment they're not husband and wife.
She likes a good gossip with Rita her friend
Of a heartache or two that they'd both like to mend.
As long as the street runs I'd just like to say
That the Rovers and Bet will be here to stay.

Irene Pearson

Coronation Street Reg

Reg is great, if not the greatest.
Problems galore, now what will be the latest?
Not another watershed,
Before he gets Maureen to bed.

Perhaps Curly will give a hand,
And take Ma-in-law to see the band,
While Reg has his lustful way;
But will Maureen come out to play?

In spite of all his past mistakes,
We know Reg has what it takes.
That joyful night, if it ever comes,
When Maureen doesn't run home to Mum's.

When Reg puts his glasses on the table,
And Maureen says: 'Are you able
To see the sight before your eyes,
Before we go to bed-y-byes?'

Please, please dear Reg do not falter;
Take a dive, but not in water.
While Ma-in-law stays hand-in-hand
With dear old Curly and that lovely band.

Alfred Cloke

Seth

Seth stands there in the Woolpack,
He's *propping up the bar.*
You may think he's not bright,
But you'd be off the mark by far.
He's canny and he's clever,
A trick just up his sleeve.
Some may come as no surprise,
And some you won't believe!
His skills are wide and varied,
Gamekeeping earns his crust.
But if hard labour you are after,
Then you won't see him for dust!
We've seen him through his triumphs,
When he's come out on top.
And we've seen his disappointments
When his plans have been a flop.
We've seen him through the good times,
When he could do no wrong
We've seen him through the bad times,
When he hasn't been so strong.
But now he's back on form,
Helping Nick make home-made wine.
Or upsetting Alan Turner,
When he finds he has the time.
There's one thing that's for certain,
We're sure of this by far.
The Woolpack wouldn't be the same
Without Seth *propping up the bar!*

I Woolhead

Jack Duckworth

Throughout the years, my hero has been
A man for all the season's
Doing this and that for *Bet the Queen*
For all his own wrong reasons

He will listen in with his best ear
To the regular's Pub chatter
Though their listeners are closed in anticipated fear
That he will volunteer his patter

His pigeons, dogs and racing fame
Leaves a lot to be desired
It's pay up, pay up and pay for the game
Leaving his pocket contents expired.

He's having to stay at Curly's gaff
To guard him from the mumps
But if Vera knows he thinks it's a laugh
He'll still end up with lumps.

Maybe the lad could have better things
As our Vera sure thinks she is royal
So, when and if the Buck House bell rings
We'll all see Jack Duckworth is loyal.

William Black

Character Bet Lynch

There is a street we've all come to know,
That happens to be the longest running show.
With a pub called the Rovers Return,
And with Bet Lynch who will never learn.

She runs the pub with such authority,
And serves the street, or the majority.
From pulling pints, to idle talk,
She swaggers in with such a walk.

She's always there with fine advice
But when it comes to men she's as cold as ice.
She'd tell you easy how to live your life,
But can't make anyone a suitable wife.

You know where you are, as Bet's so straight,
God help Jack if he turns up late.
She'll say what she thinks,
Even if it stinks.

Without Bet there'd be no street,
Kicking off our shoes putting up our feet.
To watch this soap in a week three times,
Or even to writing this poem that rhymes.

So to Bet Lynch I say to you,
Carrying on the street, that's true,
We all believe you're the best,
Certainly a cut above the rest.

Jill Stevens

Eldorado

Eldorado, a soap that was never given a chance.
Even though it got better, the public refused to glance.

Poor Ingrid, left with a baby all alone.
Living in Spain, Los Barcos, far away from home.

Trish Valentine in love with a crook.
Whisked away on to a boat, married her Captain Hook.

Joy, sad, sold her bar, got rid of her boyfriend.
Those Spanish evenings alone she will spend.

Freddie, such a warm person, always ready to give.
Minding his own business, living the way he wishes to live.

Olive King, left to try and make ends meet.
But always looking so posh and so neat.

Stanley, what have you gone and done.
Two wives at the same time, not one.

Drew wondering whatever went wrong.
Gwen telling him truth after so long.
Will they keep their marriage together.
N o matter what, they should last forever.

Marcus and Pilar of course would end up in each others arms.
Running away to an island, away from harm.

Acting was terrible at first for sure.
Then the characters grew on you more and more.
So all that is left is an empty set, everyone has gone home.
The characters are still, soon to be forgotten, Los Barcos is alone.

Deborah Hopper

No Enigma

Sharp of tongue and old of face,
Clear in voice her truths to tell.
Battling ever, somehow with grace
To admonish those who fell.

Accent strong with Northern wit,
To live and spread her personal Mission.
Eyes aglow, with stout well lit
As she fought her own submission.

Poverty written in the coat she wore,
Yet always warmth, in feelings Snug
To philosophise, but never bore,
Martha and Minnie were her drug.

Hairnet fixed, face well scrubbed,
Elsie she'd conquer with her Organ.
Never allowing that she'd be snubbed
Coronation Street's very own Gorgon.

It's some years now since she's been gone,
But in a celestial street - Ena still plays on!

Charlotte Welch

Annie of the Dales

I do like Annie Sugden
Matriarch extraordinaire
With her pickled onion lips
And her Japlacced hair.

She has ruled the Tribe of Emmerdale
Since Noah and the Flood
Her piercing eye can always spy
Each errant lamb or spud.

She's just the sort of woman
I'd really like to be
(Though Leonard, you can stay in Spain
And sorry, not with me!)

Her cooking skills are legend
She's everything that's good
She rules the roost with peck of iron
Just as roosters should.

She's strong, she's vibrant and what's more
She's had a glorious reign
But when her family misbehaved
She legged it off to Spain.

Annie is my heroine
She does the things I should
She is, in fact, the double cream
Of British womanhood!

Anne Briscoe

176

The Place to Be

Albert Square is the place to be,
Where friendly faces you will see,
Market stalls set up for the day,
A little courtyard, where children play,
The old Queen Vic pub, has pride of place,
Where people meet of every race.
Little terraced houses, joined one by one,
Small back yards, that catch the sun,
A little launderette is kept busy all day,
Where our Dot works on little pay.
But she doesn't mind or even care,
For work to find is very rare,
Everyone from the Eastend, loves Dot Cotton it's true,
She gives hope, love and charity too,
Troubles she's had, although she's shared but a few,
Her husband gone, her son Nick too,
The advice you would get, from our dear Dot,
Would be to stay grateful for all you've got
With her morals so high, her faith still kept
She is a rare breed, she has such depth
Dot if I had to describe what sort of person you are
I'd look up to the sky, and find the brightest star,
For you have a quality, like no other I know,
You shine so brightly, you let your love show.
And for that dearest Dot, I would have to say,
That's why you're loved in a very special way.

V Cowdrill

Ode to Marcus Tandy

Whose shadow flits across the scene
Whence came it from, unseen
It blights the lives of all it touches
How avoid its corrupting clutches.

His business has its many vices
Appealing and entices
Ensnaring both of friend and foe
Best not to know.

He has no *real passport* to fame
All part of the game
Behind dark shades he plans his moves
Whether or not Pilar approves.

His love for her is all consuming
Not just presuming
An inner fire burning bright
Both hearts take flight.

Marcus has an agile brain
And zest's for life in the fast lane
Fast cars and boats are his delight
He'll not give them up without a fight.

There's another aspect of his life
And in the absence of a wife
He uses his riches as he is able
One joy of his life is his riding stable.

Though his misdeeds are closing in
No restraining chains for him
The time has come to flee from Spain
By the sea, will he return again?

Although he plays a wicked part
Underneath he really is all heart.

A E Wilson

Jack Duckworth

Poor Jack, he's such a put upon man
Married to Vera what can he do?
He has no money, he has no plan,
Nothing at all to help him through.
He works as a pot man in the Rovers Return
No chance of promotion or pub of his own
His life's limited to what he can earn
To keep Vera and Tommy cosy at home.

Poor Jack, no gambling, no booze,
His specs broken and stuck up with plaster
Is this a life for a man to choose?
A man who would like to be his own master.
His son Terry is past caring
For he's locked up in jail.
No worries for him, but for Jack it's so wearing
He'll just be a burden, he'll never get bail.

Poor Jack, what does the future hold?
More work, more worry, more grief
But never the promise of gold.
A small chance of good fortune, no matter how brief
Would make him happy and make him smile
For he's stuck to Vera through thick and through thin
Although he might have quit any time
Maybe soon it will be Jack's turn to win.

Sonia E Hayes

Eldorado

I've loved Eldorado
and think it such a shame
that it is coming off the box,
the critics are too blame.

I think of you as all my friends,
and have shared your joys and woe,
now I'm feeling very sad
to have to see you go.

You brightened up the Winter
on those cold and dismal nights,
sea and sun and swimming pools
were very welcome sights.

Each and every one of you
played your part so very well,
to have to say who was the best
would be too hard to tell.

So thank you for the pleasure
you have brought for this past year,
I hoped you would be staying,
but it's not to be I fear.

I hope that in the future
we will see you all again,
your talents will be needed
if not in Sunny Spain.

Adios Amigos!

Pandora Wyatt

Davie Sneddon

If I took the High Road
To Glendarach, I would go
Just to see my Davie
And I'd like you all to know.
That I think he is the greatest thing
Since sliced bread came to being
I love his rugged handsome looks
Gives me, a real good feeling.

But bide a wie, my Davie Lad
I've some advice for you
You're not the type to want it
But it's long overdue.

Davie doesn't have much luck
In the choosing of his lovers
I think myself, he'd be better off
Taking a gander at their mothers.
Young Lynne, she's not the one for you
Watch out for your scalp, she'll have it,
She just wants a ring, a wedding ring
So watch out lad, you've had it.

She'll have you rock the cradle
Just to get her wicked way
Oh, Davie lad, forget her
You can have me, any day.

Katherine A Ford

Coronation Street

The pints are always flowing,
With Betty's cottage pie.
There's Percy Sugden moaning,
With Phyllis standing by.
Poor Jack avoiding Vera,
And all the work he can.
Ivy trying every way,
To get back with her man.
Reg and Curly dropping in,
Every now and then.
Baldwin up to all his tricks
Annoying poor old Ken.
Rita, Bet, and Mavis,
All the glamour girls.
Emily, Deirdre and Raquel
With her golden curls.
Gail and Alma, sitting there
Dreaming of the past.
Alf and Audrey making plans,
Hoping they will last.
All in all a happy place,
Where everyone can meet.
There is no place in all the world,
Like *Coronation Street*.

Doreen Ingham

Reg Holdsworth

Bettabuys would not be the same without Reg
He checks all the shelves are filled and freshens up the veg
He keeps his assistant Curly Watts on his toes
And tries to charm all the ladies wherever he goes.
He struts about the store very full of himself
But now he's rescuing Maureen from being *on the shelf*
Unfortunately for him, not everyone agrees
With his opinion that he's the *bees knees*
With his balding white hair and his enormous specs
He thinks he's irresistible to the opposite sex
He used to pester Rita in the Rovers Return
When it comes to women Reg is slow to learn.

Now, through Bettabuys he's met his future Bride
So the other women in The Street no longer need to hide
Maureen's his old flame, he's known for many years
But Reg's charm doesn't work on Mum - it falls on deaf ears.
She thinks he's a pompous fool and acts as awkward as she can
But Reg keeps on smiling to prove he's a patient man.
We hope for his sake that Maureen keeps the date
That he's set for the wedding and doesn't turn up late.
Because although he can be infuriating, you cannot ignore
The fact that he's dynamic and an asset to the store.
We wish Reg happiness with his childhood lover
And think he deserves it, as he's taking on her mother!

Barbara A Wheatley

184

The Street

The best of the soaps on the telly today
Her been running for years, rain or shine come what may.
I remember it starting a long time ago
I've laughed at the comedy, cried at the woe
Annie Walker was Queen of the Rovers back then
And for years Hilda cackled away like a hen
We loved Elsie Tanner a character great
We saw her with men out on many a date.
Ena, Minnie and Martha sat there in the snug
And Albert was there with his surly old mug.
Emily worked in a shop at the start
And heaven knows why gave old Swindley her heart.
There have been many weddings and also divorce
Some dear little babies and death came of course.
Alf's first wife Rene was hit by a car
When an iron killed Val Barlow the twins lost their ma.
Do you remember the potman named Fred
One day he appeared with a wig on his head
He wasn't a popular man I'm afraid
And when Jack took his place well then history was made.
Mike Baldwin and Ken both have grudges to bear
Since Deidre and Mike had a torrid affair.
When Bet took the Rovers things went with a bang
But who would have thought Alec Gilroy her man.
We've had Curly and Reg in the Bettabuy Store
And Steve is in trouble for breaking the law.
Poor Des has had trouble he didn't deserve
And no longer does Alf in the corner shop serve
There's Mavis and Rita but that is enough
So all I can say is the Street is great stuff.

V Cushway

Coronation Street

The day has been long, I'm beginning to tire,
Ah! a comfortable chair, a welcoming fire,
A biscuit or two, a strong cup of tea,
At last I can look at my precious TV.

Oh! Friday, of course, I can follow the Street
Percy Sugden's the man I would so like to meet,
He's always well shaven, wears a collar and tie,
The cap? I've no love for, I cannot deny.

He always means well, but things never go right
He told high-ups Bet's grub was quite a delight,
But it cost a new kitchen, an expensive job,
From the Rover's he nearly got his demob.

Love came to his life, but, as usual, no luck,
He tried to help Emily, but that came unstuck,
Writers, please change his life, how, I can't quite decide,
Wed, Emily, perhaps, have Phyllis . . . a bit on the side.

T Gardner

Oh Ken

He's led a tragic life
It really makes you weep
But if you watch him long enough
He'll send you off to sleep.

Boring Ken, they call him
The dullard in the Street
He's suffered Deidre's perm for years
But he's never been discrete.

He's had his share of women
Stretched across the years
The death, the pain, the heartache
Ken's shed so many tears.

And if that hasn't been enough,
There's been a further sin
Love triangles and daughter wed
To that cad of cads - Baldwin.

Of course the years are kind to him
He still turns a pretty head
But life above the corner shop
Is certainly no rosy bed.

One day the sun will shine on him
And fans will heave a sigh
But look out around the corner
For Baldwin acting sly.

Ken Oh Ken don't ever change
We love your tragic life
The years you've entertained us
Have been worth all the strife.

T J Smith

187